Puppet 3 Beginner's Guide

Start from scratch with the Puppet configuration
management system, and learn how to fully utilize
Puppet through simple, practical examples

John Arundel

BIRMINGHAM - MUMBAI

Puppet 3 Beginner's Guide

First published: April 2013

Production Reference: 1050413

Published by Packt Publishing Ltd.
Livery Place
35 Livery Street
Birmingham B3 2PB, UK.

ISBN 978-1-78216-124-0

www.packtpub.com

Cover Image by Faiz Fattohi (faizfattohi@gmail.com)

Credits

Author
John Arundel

Reviewers
Ugo Bellavance

Jason Slagle

Johan De Wit

Acquisition Editor
Joanne Fitzpatrick

Lead Technical Editor
Joanne Fitzpatrick

Technical Editors
Sharvari Baet

Kaustubh S. Mayekar

Project Coordinator
Anugya Khurana

Proofreader
Lawrence A. Herman

Indexer
Monica Ajmera Mehta

Graphics
Ronak Dhruv

Aditi Gajjar

Production Coordinator
Melwyn D'sa

Cover Work
Melwyn D'sa

About the Author

John Arundel is an infrastructure consultant who helps people make their computer systems more reliable, useful, and cost-effective and has fun doing it. He has what Larry Wall describes as the three great virtues of a programmer: laziness, impatience, and hubris.

Laziness, because he doesn't like doing work that a computer could do instead. Impatience, because he wants to get stuff done right away. Hubris, because he likes building systems that are as good as he can make them.

He was formerly a senior operations engineer at global telco Verizon, designing resilient, high-performance infrastructures for corporations such as Ford, McDonald's, and Bank of America. He now works independently, helping to bring enterprise-grade performance and reliability to clients with slightly smaller pockets but very big ideas.

He likes writing books, especially about Puppet. It seems that at least some people enjoy reading them, or maybe they just like the pictures. He also occasionally provides training and coaching on Puppet, which turns out to be far harder than simply doing the work himself.

Off the clock, he can usually be found driving a Land Rover up some mountain or other. He lives in a small cottage in Cornwall and believes, like Cicero, that if you have a garden and a library, then you have everything you need.

You can follow him on Twitter at `@bitfield`.

Thanks are due to my friend Luke Kanies, who created a configuration management tool that sucks less, and also to the many proofreaders and contributors to this book, including Andy Brockhurst, Tim Eilers, Martin Ellis, Adam Garside, Stefan Goethals, Jennifer Harbison, Kanthi Kiran, Cristian Leonte, Habeeb Rahman, John Smith, Sebastiaan van Steenis, Jeff Sussna, Nate Walck, Bryan Weber, and Matt Willsher.

About the Reviewers

Ugo Bellavance has done most of his studies in e-commerce, started using Linux at Red Hat 5.2, got Linux training from Savoir-Faire-Linux at the age of 20, and got his RHCE on RHEL 6 in 2011. He's been a consultant in the past, but he's now an employee for a provincial government agency for which he manages the infrastructure (servers, workstations, network, security, virtualization, SAN/NAS, PBX). He's a big fan of open-source software and its underlying philosophy. He's worked with Debian, Ubuntu, and SUSE, but what he knows best is RHEL-based distributions. He's known for his contributions to the MailScanner project (he has been a technical reviewer for the MailScanner book), but he also gave time to different open-source projects, such as mondorescue, OTRS, SpamAssassin, pfSense, and a few others.

I thank my lover, Lysanne, who accepted allowing me some free time slots for this review even with a 2-year-old and a 6-month-old to take care of. The presence of these 3 human beings in my life is simply invaluable.

I must also thank my friend Sébastien, whose generosity is only matched by his knowledge and kindness. I would never have reached that high in my career if it wasn't for him.

Jason Slagle is a 15-year veteran of Systems and Network administration. Having worked on everything from Linux systems to Cisco networks and SAN Storage, he is always looking for ways to make his work repeatable and automated. When he is not hacking at a computer for work or pleasure, he enjoys running, cycling, and occasionally geocaching.

He is currently employed by CNWR, Inc., an IT and Infrastructure consulting company in his home town of Toledo, Ohio. There he supports several larger customers in their quest to automate and improve their infrastructure and development operations.

> I'd like to thank my wife, Heather, for being patient through the challenges of being married to a lifelong systems guy, and my new son, Jacob, for bringing a smile to my face on even the longest days.

Johan De Wit was an early Linux user and he still remembers those days building a 0.9x Linux kernel on his brand-new 486 computer that took a whole night, and always had a great love for the UNIX Operating System.

It is not surprising that he started a career as a UNIX system administrator.

Since 2009, he has been working as an open-source consultant at Open-Future, where he got the opportunity to work with Puppet. Right now, Puppet has become Johan's biggest interest, and recently he became a Puppet trainer.

Besides his work with Puppet, he spends a lot of his free time with his two lovely kids and his two Belgian draft horses, and if time and the weather permit, he likes to drive his chopper.

www.PacktPub.com

Support files, eBooks, discount offers and more

You might want to visit www.PacktPub.com for support files and downloads related to your book.

Did you know that Packt offers eBook versions of every book published, with PDF and ePub files available? You can upgrade to the eBook version at www.PacktPub.com and as a print book customer, you are entitled to a discount on the eBook copy. Get in touch with us at service@packtpub.com for more details.

At www.PacktPub.com, you can also read a collection of free technical articles, sign up for a range of free newsletters and receive exclusive discounts and offers on Packt books and eBooks.

http://PacktLib.PacktPub.com

Do you need instant solutions to your IT questions? PacktLib is Packt's online digital book library. Here, you can access, read and search across Packt's entire library of books.

Why Subscribe?

- Fully searchable across every book published by Packt
- Copy and paste, print and bookmark content
- On demand and accessible via web browser

Free Access for Packt account holders

If you have an account with Packt at www.PacktPub.com, you can use this to access PacktLib today and view nine entirely free books. Simply use your login credentials for immediate access.

Table of Contents

Preface

If you work with computer systems, then you know how time-consuming it can be to install and configure software, to do administration tasks such as backups and user management, and to keep the machines up to date with security patches and new releases. Maybe you've already come up with some written procedures, shell scripts, and other ways to document your work and make it more automated and reliable.

Perhaps you've read about how Puppet can help with this, but aren't sure how to get started. The online documentation is great for reference, but doesn't really explain the whole thing from scratch. Many of the books and tutorials available spend a lot of time explaining how to set up your Puppet server and infrastructure before ever getting to the point where you can use Puppet to actually do something.

In my work as an infrastructure consultant I do a good deal of Puppet training, mostly for absolute beginners, and I've found that the most effective and fun way to do this is to get into some real work right away. In the first five minutes, I have people making changes to their systems using Puppet. If there was a fire alarm and we had to terminate the class after that first five minutes, they would still go away knowing something useful that could help them in their jobs.

I've taken the same approach in this book. Without going into lots of theory or background detail, I'll show you how to do useful things with Puppet right away: install packages and config files, create users, set up scheduled jobs, and so on. Every exercise deals with something real and practical that you're likely to need in your work, and you'll see the complete Puppet code to make it happen, along with step-by-step instructions for what to type and what output you'll see.

After each exercise, I'll explain in detail what each line of code does and how it works, so that you can adapt it to your own purposes, and feel confident that you understand everything that's happened. By the end of the book, you will have all the skills you need to do real, useful, everyday work with Puppet.

So let's get started.

What this book covers

Chapter 1, Introduction to Puppet, explains the problem of configuration management and why traditional manual approaches to them don't scale. It shows how Puppet deals with these problems efficiently, and introduces the basic architecture of Puppet.

Chapter 2, First Steps with Puppet, guides you through installing Puppet for the first time, creating a simple manifest, and applying it to a machine. You'll see how to use the Puppet language to describe and modify resources, such as a text file.

Chapter 3, Packages, Files, and Services, shows you how to use these key resource types, and how they work together. We'll work through a complete and useful example based on the Nginx web server.

Chapter 4, Managing Puppet with Git, describes a simple and powerful way to connect machines together using Puppet, and to distribute your manifests and work on them collaboratively using the version control system Git.

Chapter 5, Managing Users, outlines some good practices for user administration and shows how to use Puppet to implement them. You'll also see how to control access using SSH and manage user privileges using `sudo`.

Chapter 6, Tasks and Templates, covers more key aspects of automation: scheduling tasks, and building configuration files from dynamic data using Puppet's template mechanism.

Chapter 7, Definitions and Classes, builds on previous chapters by showing you how to organize Puppet code into reusable modules and objects. We'll see how to create definitions and classes, and how to pass parameters to them.

Chapter 8, Expressions and Logic, delves into the Puppet language and shows how to control flow using conditional statements and logical expressions, and how to build arithmetic and string expressions. It also covers operators, arrays, and hashes.

Chapter 9, Reporting and Troubleshooting, looks at the practical side of working with Puppet: how to diagnose and solve common problems, debugging Puppet's operations, and understanding Puppet error messages.

Chapter 10, Moving on Up, shows you how to make your Puppet code more elegant, more readable, and more maintainable. It offers some links and suggestions for further reading, and outlines a series of practical projects that will help you deliver measurable business value using Puppet.

What you need for this book

You'll need a computer system (preferably, but not essentially, Ubuntu Linux-based) and access to the Internet. You won't need to be a UNIX expert or an experienced sysadmin; I'll assume you can log in, run commands, and edit files, but otherwise I'll explain everything you need as we go.

Who this book is for

This book is aimed at system administrators, developers, and others who need to do system administration, who have grasped the basics of working with the command line, editing files, and so on, but want to learn how to use Puppet to get more done, and make their lives easier.

Conventions

In this book, you will find several headings appearing frequently.

To give clear instructions on how to complete a procedure or task, we use:

Time for action – heading

1. Action 1
2. Action 2
3. Action 3

Instructions often need some extra explanation to make sense, so they are followed with:

What just happened?

This heading explains the working of tasks or instructions that you have just completed.

You will also find some other learning aids in the book, including:

Pop quiz – heading

These are short multiple-choice questions intended to help you test your own understanding.

Have a go hero – heading

These practical challenges give you ideas for experimenting with what you have learned.

You will also find a number of styles of text that distinguish between different kinds of information. Here are some examples of these styles, and an explanation of their meaning.

Code words in text, database table names, folder names, filenames, file extensions, pathnames, dummy URLs, user input, and Twitter handles are shown as follows: "To have Puppet read a manifest file and apply it to the server, use the `puppet apply` command."

A block of code is set as follows:

```
file { '/tmp/hello':
  content => "Hello, world\n",
}
```

When we wish to draw your attention to a particular part of a code block, the relevant lines or items are set in bold:

```
file { '/tmp/hello':
  content => "Hello, world\n",
}
```

Any command-line input or output is written as follows:

```
ubuntu@demo:~$ puppet apply site.pp
Notice: /Stage[main]//Node[demo]/File[/tmp/hello]/ensure: defined content
as '{md5}bc6e6f16b8a077ef5fbc8d59d0b931b9'
Notice: Finished catalog run in 0.05 seconds
```

New terms and **important words** are shown in bold. Words that you see on the screen, in menus or dialog boxes for example, appear in the text like this: "On the **Select Destination Location** screen, click on **Next** to accept the default destination."

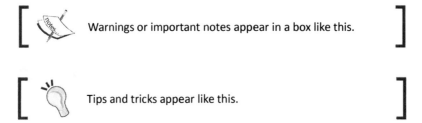

Warnings or important notes appear in a box like this.

Tips and tricks appear like this.

Reader feedback

Feedback from our readers is always welcome. Let us know what you think about this book—what you liked or may have disliked. Reader feedback is important for us to develop titles that you really get the most out of.

To send us general feedback, simply send an e-mail to `feedback@packtpub.com`, and mention the book title in the subject of your message.

If there is a topic that you have expertise in and you are interested in either writing or contributing to a book, see our author guide at `www.packtpub.com/authors`.

Customer support

Now that you are the proud owner of a Packt book, we have a number of things to help you to get the most from your purchase.

Errata

Although we have taken every care to ensure the accuracy of our content, mistakes do happen. If you find a mistake in one of our books—maybe a mistake in the text or the code—we would be grateful if you would report this to us. By doing so, you can save other readers from frustration and help us improve subsequent versions of this book. If you find any errata, please report them by visiting `http://www.packtpub.com/submit-errata`, selecting your book, clicking on the **errata submission form** link, and entering the details of your errata. Once your errata are verified, your submission will be accepted and the errata will be uploaded to our website, or added to any list of existing errata, under the Errata section of that title.

Piracy

Piracy of copyright material on the Internet is an ongoing problem across all media. At Packt, we take the protection of our copyright and licenses very seriously. If you come across any illegal copies of our works, in any form, on the Internet, please provide us with the location address, or website name immediately so that we can pursue a remedy.

Please contact us at `copyright@packtpub.com` with a link to the suspected pirated material.

We appreciate your help in protecting our authors, and our ability to bring you valuable content.

Questions

You can contact us at `questions@packtpub.com` if you are having a problem with any aspect of the book, and we will do our best to address it.

Introduction to Puppet

For a list of all the ways technology has failed to improve the quality of life, please press three.

— Alice Kahn

In this chapter, you'll learn what Puppet is, and what it can help you do. Whether you're a system administrator, a developer who needs to fix servers from time to time, or just someone who's annoyed at how long it takes to set up a new laptop, you'll have come across the kind of problems that Puppet is designed to solve.

The problem

We have the misfortune to be living in the present. In the future, of course, computers will be smart enough to just figure out what we want, and do it. Until then, we have to spend a lot of time telling telling the computer things it should already know.

When you buy a new laptop, you can't just plug it in, get your e-mail, and start work. You have to tell it your name, your e-mail address, the address of your ISP's e-mail servers, and so on.

Also, you need to install the programs you use: your preferred web browser, word processor, and so on. Some of this software may need license keys. Your various logins and accounts need passwords. You have to set all the preferences up the way you're used to.

This is a tedious process. How long does it take you to get from a box-fresh computer to being productive? For me, it probably takes about a week to get things just as I want them. It's all the little details.

Configuration management

This problem is called **configuration management**, and thankfully we don't have it with a new laptop too often. But imagine multiplying it by fifty or a hundred computers, and setting them all up manually.

When I started out as a system administrator, that's pretty much what I did. A large part of my time was spent configuring server machines and making them ready for use. This is more or less the same process as setting up a new laptop: installing software, licensing it, configuring it, setting passwords, and so on.

A day in the life of a sysadmin

Let's look at some of the tasks involved in preparing a web server, which is something sysadmins do pretty often. I'll use a fictitious, but all too plausible, website as an example. Congratulations: you're in charge of setting up the server for an exciting, innovative social media application called `cat-pictures.com`.

Assuming the machine has been physically put together, racked, cabled, and powered, and the operating system is installed, what do we have to do to make it usable as a server for `cat-pictures.com`?

- Add some user accounts and passwords
- Configure security settings and privileges
- Install all the packages needed to run the application

- Customize the configuration files for each of these packages

- Create databases and database user accounts; load some initial data

- Configure the services that should be running

- Deploy the `cat-pictures` application

- Add some necessary files: uploaded cat pictures, for example

- Configure the machine for monitoring

That's a lot of work. It may take a day or two if this is the first time you're setting up the server. If you're smart, you'll write down everything you do, so next time you can simply run through the steps and copy and paste all the commands you need. Even so, the next time you build a `cat-pictures` server, it'll still take you a couple of hours to do this.

If the live server goes down and you suddenly need to build a replacement, that's a couple of hours of downtime, and with a pointy-haired boss yelling at you, it's a bad couple of hours.

Wouldn't it be nice if you could write a specification of how the server should be set up, and you could apply it to as many machines as you liked?

Keeping the configuration synchronized

So the first problem with building servers by hand (**artisan server crafting**, as it's been called) is that it's complicated and tedious and it takes a long time. There's another problem. The next time you need to build an identical server, how do you do it?

Your painstaking notes will no longer be up to date with reality. While you were on vacation, the developers installed a couple of new Ruby gems that the application now depends on—I guess they forgot to tell you. Even if everybody keeps the build document up to date with changes, no one actually tests the modified build process, so there's no way to know if it still works end-to-end.

Also, the latest version of MySQL in the Linux distribution has changed, and now it doesn't support some of the configuration parameters you used before. So the differences start to accumulate.

By the time you've got four or five servers, they're all a little different. Which is the authoritative one? Or are they all slightly wrong? The longer they're around, the more they will drift apart.

Wouldn't it be nice if the configuration on all your machines could be regularly checked and synchronized with a central, standard version?

Repeating changes across many servers

The latest feature on `cat-pictures.com` is that people can now upload movies of their cats doing adorable things. To roll out the new version to your five web servers, you need to install a couple of new package dependencies and change a configuration file. And you need to do this same process on each machine.

Humans just aren't good at accurately repeating complex tasks over and over; that's why we invented robots. It's easy to make mistakes, leave things out, or be interrupted and lose track of what you've done.

Changes happen all the time, and it becomes increasingly difficult to keep things up to date and in sync as your infrastructure grows.

Wouldn't it be nice if you only had to make changes in one place, and they rolled out to your whole network automatically?

Self-updating documentation

A new sysadmin joins your organization, and she needs to know where all the servers are, and what they do. Even if you keep scrupulous documentation, it can't always be relied on. In real life, we're too busy to stop every five minutes and document what we just did.

The only accurate documentation, in fact, is the servers themselves. You can look at a server to see how it's configured, but that only applies while you still have the machine. If something goes wrong and you can't access the machine, or the data on it, your only option is to reconstruct the lost configuration from scratch.

Wouldn't it be nice if you had a configuration document which was guaranteed to be up to date?

Coping with different platforms

Ideally, all your machines would have the same hardware and the same operating system. If only things were that easy. What usually happens is that we have a mix of different types of machines and different operating systems and we have to know about all of them.

The command to create a new user account is slightly different for Red Hat Linux from the equivalent command for Ubuntu, for example. Solaris is a little different again. Each command is doing basically the same job, but has differences in syntax, arguments, and default values.

This means that any attempt to automate user management across your network has to take account of all these differences, and if you add another platform to the mix, then that further increases the complexity of the code required to handle it.

Wouldn't it be nice if you could just say how things should be, and not worry about the details of how to make it happen?

Version control and history

Sometimes you start trying to fix a problem and instead make things worse. Or things were working yesterday, and you want to go back to the way things were then. Sorry, no do-overs.

When you're making manual, ad hoc changes to systems, you can't roll back to a point in time. It's hard to undo a whole series of changes. You don't have a way of keeping track of what you did and how things changed.

This is bad enough if there's just one of you. When you're working in a team, it gets even worse, with everybody making independent changes and getting in each other's way.

When you have a problem, you need a way to know what changed, and when, and who did it. Ideally, you could look at your configuration document and say, "Hmm, Carol checked in a change to the FTP server last night, and today no one can log in. It looks like she made a typo." You can fix or back out of the change, and have Carol buy the team lunch.

Wouldn't it be nice if you could go back in time?

Solving the problem

Most of us have tried to solve these problems of configuration management in various ways. Some write shell scripts to automate builds and installs, some use makefiles to generate configurations, some use templates and disk images, and so on. Often these techniques are combined with version control, to solve the history problem. Systems like these can be quite effective, and even a little bit of automation is much better than none.

Reinventing the wheel

The disadvantage with this kind of home-brewed solution is that each sysadmin has to reinvent the wheel, often many times. The ways in which organizations solve the configuration management problem are usually proprietary and highly site-specific. So for every new place you work, you need to build a new **configuration management system (CM system)**.

Because everyone has his own proprietary, unique system, the skills associated with it aren't transferable. When you get a new job, all the time and effort you spent becoming a wizard on your organization's CM system goes to waste; you have to learn a new one.

A waste of effort

Also, there's a whole lot of duplicated effort. The world really doesn't need more template engines, for example. Once a decent one exists, it would make sense for everybody to use it, and take advantage of ongoing improvements and updates.

It's not just the CM system itself that represents duplicated, wasted effort. The configuration scripts and templates you write could also be shared and improved by others, if only they had access to them. After all, most server software is pretty widely used. A program in configuration language that sets up Apache could be used by everybody who uses Apache—if it were a standard language.

Transferable skills

Once you have a CM system with a critical mass of users, you get a lot of benefits. A new system administrator doesn't have to write his own CM tool, he just grabs one off the shelf. Once he learns to use it, and to write programs in the standard language, he can take that skill with him to other jobs.

He can choose from a large library of existing programs in the standard configuration language, covering most of the popular software in use. These programs are updated and improved to keep up with changes in the software and operating systems they manage.

This kind of beneficial network effect is why we don't have a million different operating systems, or programming languages, or processor chips. There's strong pressure for people to converge on a standard. On the other hand, we don't have just one of each of those things either. There's never just one solution that pleases everybody.

If you're not happy with an existing CM system, and you have the skills, you can write one that works the way you prefer. If enough other people feel the same way, they will form a critical mass of users for the new system. But this won't happen indefinitely; standardization pressure means the market will tend to converge on a small number of competing systems.

Configuration management tools

This is roughly the situation we have now. Several different CM systems have been developed over the years, with new ones coming along all the time, but only a few have achieved significant market share. At the time of writing, at least for UNIX-like systems, these CM systems are Puppet, Chef, and CFEngine.

There really isn't much to choose between these different systems. They all solve more or less the same problems—the ones we saw earlier in this chapter—in more or less the same way. Some people prefer the Puppet way of doing things; some people are more comfortable with Chef, and so on.

But essentially, these, and many other CM systems, are all great solutions to the CM problem, and it's not very important which one you choose as long as you choose one.

Infrastructure as code

Once we start writing programs to configure machines, we get some benefits right away. We can adopt the tools and techniques that regular programmers—who write code in Ruby or Java, for example—have used for years:

◆ Powerful editing and refactoring tools

◆ Version control

◆ Tests

◆ Pair programming

◆ Code reviews

This can make us more agile and flexible as system administrators, able to deal with fast-changing requirements and deliver things quickly to the business. We can also produce higher-quality, more reliable work.

Dawn of the devop

Some of the benefits are more subtle, organizational, and psychological. There is often a divide between "devs", who wrangle code, and "ops", who wrangle configuration. Traditionally, the skill sets of the two groups haven't overlapped much. It was common until recently for system administrators not to write complex programs, and for developers to have little or no experience of building and managing servers.

That's changing fast. System administrators, facing the challenge of scaling systems to enormous size for the web, have had to get smart about programming and automation. Developers, who now often build applications, services, and businesses by themselves, couldn't do what they do without knowing how to set up and fix servers.

The term "devops" has begun to be used to describe the growing overlap between these skill sets. It can mean sysadmins who happily turn their hand to writing code when needed, or developers who don't fear the command line, or it can simply mean the people for whom the distinction is no longer useful.

Devops write code, herd servers, build apps, scale systems, analyze outages, and fix bugs. With the advent of CM systems, devs and ops are now all just people who work with code.

Job satisfaction

Being a sysadmin, in the traditional sense, is not usually a very exciting job. Instead of getting to apply your experience and ingenuity to make things better, faster, and more reliable, you spend a lot of time just fixing problems, and making manual configuration changes that could really be done by a machine. The following carefully-researched diagram shows how traditional system administration compares to some other jobs in both excitement and stress levels:

We can see from this that manual sysadmin work is both more stressful and more boring than we would like. Boring, because you're not really using your brain, and stressful, because things keep going wrong despite your best efforts.

Automating at least some of the dull manual work can make sysadmin work more exciting, because it frees you for things that are more important and challenging, such as figuring out how to make your systems more resilient or more performant.

Having an automated infrastructure means your servers are consistent, up to date, and well-documented, so it can also make your job a little less stressful. Or, at any rate, it can give you the freedom to be stressed about more interesting things.

The Puppet advantage

So how do you do system administration with Puppet? Well, it turns out, not too differently from the way you already do it. But because Puppet handles the low-level details of creating users, installing packages, and so on, you're now free to think about your configuration at a slightly higher level.

Let's look at an example sysadmin task and see how it's handled the traditional way and then the Puppet way.

Welcome aboard

A new developer has joined the organization. She needs a user account on all the servers. The traditional approach will be as follows:

1. Log in to server 1.

2. Run the `useradd rachel` command to create the new user.

3. Create Rachel's home directory.

4. Log in to server 2 and repeat these steps.

5. Log in to server 3 and repeat these steps.

6. Log in to server 4 and repeat these steps.

7. Log in to server 5 and repeat these steps.

8. The first three steps will be repeated for all the servers.

The Puppet way

Here's what you might do to achieve the same result in a typical Puppet-powered infrastructure:

Add the following lines to your Puppet code:

```
user { 'rachel':
  ensure => present,
}
```

Puppet runs automatically a few minutes later on all your machines and picks up the change you made. It checks the list of users on the machine, and if Rachel isn't on the list, Puppet will take action. It detects what kind of operating system is present and knows what commands need to be run in that environment to add a user. After Puppet has completed its work, the list of users on the machine will match the ones in your Puppet code.

The key differences from the traditional, manual approach are as follows:

- You only had to specify the steps to create a new user once, instead of doing them every time for each new user

- You only had to add the user in one place, instead of on every machine in your infrastructure

- You didn't have to worry about the OS-specific details of how to add users

Growing your network

It's not hard to see that, if you have more than a couple of servers, the Puppet way scales much better than the traditional way. Years ago, perhaps many companies would have had only one or two servers. Nowadays it's common for a single infrastructure to have tens or even hundreds of servers.

By the time you've got to, say, five servers, the Puppet advantage is obvious. Not counting the initial investment in setting up Puppet, you're getting things done five times faster. Your colleague doing things the traditional, hand-crafted way is still only on machine number 2 by the time you're heading home.

Above ten servers the traditional approach becomes almost unmanageable. You spend most of your time simply doing repetitive tasks over and over just to keep up with changes. To look at it in another, more commercial way, your firm needs ten sysadmins to get as much work done as one person with Puppet.

Cloud scaling

Beyond ten or so servers, there simply isn't a choice. You can't manage an infrastructure like this by hand. If you're using a cloud computing architecture, where servers are created and destroyed minute-by-minute in response to changing demand, the artisan approach to server crafting just won't work.

What is Puppet?

We've seen the problems that Puppet solves, and how it solves them, by letting you express the way your servers should be configured in code form. Puppet itself is an interpreter that reads those descriptions (written in the Puppet language) and makes configuration changes on a machine so that it conforms to your specification.

The Puppet language

What does this language look like? It's not a series of instructions, such as a shell script or a Ruby program. It's more like a set of declarations about the way things should be:

```
package { 'curl':
  ensure => installed,
}
```

In English, this code says, "The curl package should be installed". This snippet of code results in Puppet doing the following:

 ◆ Checking the list of installed packages to see if curl is already installed

 ◆ If not, installing it

Another example is as follows:

```
user { 'jen':
  ensure => present,
}
```

This is Puppet language for the declaration "The `jen` user should be present." Again, this results in Puppet checking for the existence of the `jen` user on the system, and creating it if necessary.

So you can see that the Puppet program—the Puppet **manifest**—for your configuration is a set of declarations about what things should exist, and how they should be configured.

You don't give commands, such as "Do this, then do that." Rather, you describe how things should be, and let Puppet take care of making it happen. These are two quite different kinds of programming. The first (**procedural** style) is the traditional model used by languages, such as C, Python, shell, and so on. Puppet's is called **declarative** style because you declare what the end result should be, rather than specifying the steps to get there.

This means that you can apply the same Puppet manifest repeatedly to a machine and the end result will be the same, no matter how many times you run the "program". It's better to think of Puppet manifests as a kind of executable specification rather than as a program in the traditional sense.

Resources and attributes

This is powerful because the same manifest—"The `curl` package should be installed and the `jen` user should be present"—can be applied to different machines all running different operating systems.

Puppet lets you describe configuration in terms of **resources**—what things should exist—and their **attributes**. You don't have to get into the details of how resources are created and configured on different platforms. Puppet just takes care of it.

Here are some of the kinds of resources you can describe in Puppet:

- Packages
- Files
- Services
- Users
- Groups
- YUM repos
- Nagios configuration

- Log messages
- `/etc/hosts` entries
- Network interfaces
- SSH keys
- SELinux settings
- Kerberos configuration
- ZFS attributes
- E-mail aliases
- Mailing lists
- Mounted filesystems
- Scheduled jobs
- VLANs
- Solaris zones

In fact, since you can define custom resources to manage anything that's not covered by the built-in resources, there are no limits. Puppet allows you to automate every possible aspect of system configuration.

Summary

A quick rundown of what we've learned in this chapter.

Configuration management

Manual **configuration management** is tedious and repetitive, it's error-prone, and it doesn't scale well. Puppet is a tool for automating this process.

You describe your configuration in terms of **resources** such as packages and files. This description is called a **manifest**.

What Puppet does

When Puppet runs on a computer, it compares the current configuration to the manifest. It will take whatever actions are needed to change the machine so that it matches the manifest.

Puppet supports a wide range of different platforms and operating systems, and it will automatically run the appropriate commands to apply your manifest in each environment.

The Puppet advantage

Using Puppet addresses a number of key problems with manual configuration management:

- You can write a manifest once and apply it to many machines, avoiding duplicated work

- You can keep all your servers in sync with each other, and with the manifest

- The Puppet manifest also acts as live documentation, which is guaranteed to be up to date

- Puppet copes with differences between operating systems, platforms, command syntaxes, and so on

- Because Puppet manifests are code, you can version and manage them in the same way as any other source code

Scaling

The problems with manual configuration management become acute when your infrastructure scales to 5-10 servers. Beyond that, especially when you're operating in the cloud where servers can be created and destroyed in response to changing demand, some way of **automating** your configuration management is essential.

The Puppet language

Puppet manifests are written in a special language for describing system configuration. This language defines units called **resources**, each of which describes some aspect of the system: a user, a file, a software package, and so on:

```
package { 'curl':
  ensure => installed,
}
```

Puppet is a **declarative** programming language: that is, it describes how things should be, rather than listing a series of actions to take, as in some other programming languages, such as Perl or shell. Puppet compares the current state of a server to its manifest, and changes only those things that don't match. This means you can run Puppet as many times as you want and the end result will be the same.

2

First steps with Puppet

Beginnings are such delicate times.

> — Frank Herbert, "Dune"

In this chapter you'll learn how to install Puppet, how to write your first manifest, and how to put Puppet to work configuring a server. You'll also understand how Puppet reads and applies a manifest.

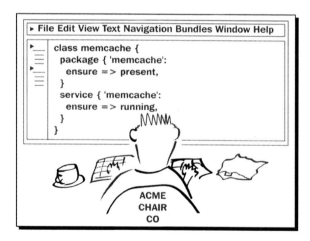

What you'll need

To follow the examples in this chapter, you'll need a computer, preferably running Linux, connected to the Internet. You'll also need to be able to run commands in a terminal and do simple editing of the text files. You'll also need to be able to acquire root-level access via sudo.

Although Puppet runs on a number of different platforms, I'm not going to provide detailed instructions for all of them. Throughout this book I'll be using the Ubuntu 12.04 LTS "Precise" distribution of Linux for my examples. I'll point out where specific commands or file locations are likely to be different for other operating systems.

I'm using an Amazon EC2 cloud instance to demonstrate setting up Puppet, though you may prefer to use a physical server, a Linux workstation, or a Vagrant virtual machine (with Internet access). I'll log in as the Ubuntu user and use sudo to run commands that need root privileges (the default setup on Ubuntu).

Time for action – preparing for Puppet

We need to do a few things to make the server ready for installing Puppet.

1. Set a suitable hostname for your server (ignore any warning from sudo):

    ```
    ubuntu@domU-12-31-39-09-51-23:~$ sudo hostname demo
    ubuntu@domU-12-31-39-09-51-23:~$ sudo su -c 'echo demo >/etc/
    hostname'
    sudo: unable to resolve host demo
    ```

2. Log out and log back in to check that the hostname is now correctly set:

    ```
    ubuntu@demo:~$
    ```

3. Find out the local IP address of the server:

    ```
    ubuntu@demo:~$ ip addr list |grep eth0$
        inet 10.210.86.209/23 brd 10.210.87.255 scope global eth0
    ```

4. Copy the IP address of your server (here it's 10.210.86.209) and add this to the /etc/hosts file (use your own hostname and domain):

    ```
    ubuntu@demo:~$ sudo su -c 'echo 10.210.86.209 demo demo.example.
    com >>/etc/hosts'
    sudo: unable to resolve host demo
    ```

Time for action – installing Puppet

You can get a Puppet package for most Linux distributions from Puppet Labs. Here's how to install the package for Ubuntu 12.04 Precise:

1. Download and install the Puppet Labs repo package as follows:

```
ubuntu@demo:~$ wget http://apt.puppetlabs.com/puppetlabs-release-
precise.deb

--2013-01-09 13:38:24--  http://apt.puppetlabs.com/puppetlabs-
release-precise.deb

Resolving apt.puppetlabs.com (apt.puppetlabs.com)...
96.126.116.126, 2600:3c00::f03c:91ff:fe93:711a

Connecting to apt.puppetlabs.com (apt.puppetlabs.
com)|96.126.116.126|:80... connected.

HTTP request sent, awaiting response... 200 OK

Length: 3392 (3.3K) [application/x-debian-package]

Saving to: `puppetlabs-release-precise.deb'


100%[======================================>] 3,392        --.-K/s
in 0.001s


2013-01-09 13:38:25 (2.54 MB/s) - `puppetlabs-release-precise.deb'
saved [3392/3392]


ubuntu@demo:~$ sudo dpkg -i puppetlabs-release-precise.deb
Selecting previously unselected package puppetlabs-release.
(Reading database ... 33153 files and directories currently
installed.)
Unpacking puppetlabs-release (from puppetlabs-release-precise.deb)
...
Setting up puppetlabs-release (1.0-5) ...
```

2. Update your APT configuration as follows:

```
ubuntu@demo:~$ sudo apt-get update
Ign http://us-east-1.ec2.archive.ubuntu.com precise InRelease
Ign http://us-east-1.ec2.archive.ubuntu.com precise-updates
InRelease
Get:1 http://us-east-1.ec2.archive.ubuntu.com precise Release.gpg
[198 B]
Get:2 http://us-east-1.ec2.archive.ubuntu.com precise-updates
Release.gpg [198 B]
```

```
Ign http://apt.puppetlabs.com precise InRelease
Get:3 http://apt.puppetlabs.com precise Release.gpg [836 B]
Get:4 http://apt.puppetlabs.com precise Release [8,859 B]
...
Fetched 12.6 MB in 6s (1,943 kB/s)
Reading package lists... Done
```

 You can find out how to configure your particular system for the Puppet Labs repos at the following page:

http://docs.puppetlabs.com/guides/puppetlabs_
package_repositories.html

3. Install Puppet as follows:

```
ubuntu@demo:~$ sudo apt-get -y install puppet
Reading package lists... Done
Building dependency tree
Reading state information... Done
The following extra packages will be installed:
  augeas-lenses debconf-utils facter hiera libaugeas-ruby1.8
libaugeas0
  libjson-ruby libreadline5 libruby libruby1.8 libshadow-ruby1.8
puppet-common
  ruby ruby-json ruby1.8
Suggested packages:
  augeas-doc augeas-tools puppet-el vim-puppet libselinux-ruby1.8
ruby-selinux
  librrd-ruby1.8 librrd-ruby1.9 ri ruby-dev ruby1.8-examples ri1.8
Recommended packages:
  rdoc
The following NEW packages will be installed:
  augeas-lenses debconf-utils facter hiera libaugeas-ruby1.8
libaugeas0
  libjson-ruby libreadline5 libruby libruby1.8 libshadow-ruby1.8
puppet
  puppet-common ruby ruby-json ruby1.8
0 upgraded, 16 newly installed, 0 to remove and 76 not upgraded.
Need to get 3,428 kB of archives.
After this operation, 12.2 MB of additional disk space will be
```

```
used.

Get:1 http://us-east-1.ec2.archive.ubuntu.com/ubuntu/ precise/main
libreadline5 amd64 5.2-11 [128 kB]

...

Setting up puppet (3.0.2-1puppetlabs1) ...

 * Starting puppet agent

puppet not configured to start, please edit /etc/default/puppet to
enable


[ OK ]

Processing triggers for libc-bin ...

ldconfig deferred processing now taking place
```

If you're using Red Hat Enterprise Linux, CentOS, or another Linux distribution that uses the Yum package system, you should run $ `sudo yum install puppet` to install Puppet.

If you're on a Mac, you can download and install suitable DMG images from Puppet Labs:

`https://downloads.puppetlabs.com/mac/`

If you're using Windows, you can download the MSI packages from the Puppet Labs website:

`https://downloads.puppetlabs.com/windows/`

4. Run the following command to check that Puppet is properly installed:

```
ubuntu@demo:~$ puppet --version
3.0.2
```

If the version of Puppet you've installed is not exactly the same, it doesn't matter; you'll get whatever is the latest version made available by Puppet Labs. If you're installing Puppet from a different place, or from source files, then as long as your version is newer than 3.0, you'll have no trouble running the examples in this book.

If you have a version of Puppet that is older (for example, Puppet 2.6 or 2.7) you may find that some things don't work or work differently from the way you'd expect. Many changes in syntax that were deprecated in older versions, for example, no longer work at all in Puppet 3.0. I recommend that you upgrade to Puppet 3.0 or later if at all possible.

Your first manifest

To see what Puppet code looks like, and how Puppet makes changes to a machine, we'll create a manifest file and have Puppet apply it.

Create the file `site.pp` anywhere you like, with the following contents:

```
file { '/tmp/hello':
  content => "Hello, world\n",
}
```

How it works

You can probably guess what this manifest will do, but I'll explain the code in detail first.

```
file { '/tmp/hello':
```

The word `file` begins a **resource** declaration for a file resource. Recall that a resource is some bit of configuration that you want Puppet to manage: for example, a file, user account, or package. A resource declaration looks like this:

```
RESOURCE { NAME:
  ATTRIBUTE => VALUE,
  ...
}
```

`RESOURCE` indicates the type of resource you're declaring; in this case, it's a `file`.

`NAME` is a unique identifier that distinguishes this instance of the resource from any other that Puppet knows about. With file resources, it's usual for this to be the full path to the file, in this case, `/tmp/hello`.

There follows a list of **attributes** that describe how the resource should be configured. The attributes available depend on the type of resource. For a file, you can set attributes such as `content`, `owner`, `group`, and `mode`.

```
content => "Hello, world\n",
```

The `content` attribute sets the contents of a file to a string value you provide. Here, the contents of the file are declared to be `Hello, world` followed by a newline character.

Note that `content` specifies the entire content of the file; the string you provide will replace anything already in the file, rather than being appended to it.

Applying the manifest

To have Puppet read a manifest file, apply it to the server, and use the `puppet apply` command.

Run the following command in the same directory where you created `site.pp`:

```
ubuntu@demo:~$ puppet apply site.pp
Notice: /Stage[main]//Node[demo]/File[/tmp/hello]/ensure: defined
content as '{md5}bc6e6f16b8a077ef5fbc8d59d0b931b9'
Notice: Finished catalog run in 0.05 seconds
```

What just happened?

Here's how your manifest is processed. First, Puppet reads the manifest file and the list of resources it contains (in this case, there's just one resource).

Puppet then works through the list, applying each resource in turn:

◆ First, it checks if the resource exists on the server. If not, Puppet creates it.

◆ In the example, we've declared that the file `/tmp/hello` should exist. The first time you run `puppet apply`, this won't be the case, so Puppet will create the file for you.

◆ Then, for each resource, it checks the value of each attribute in the manifest against what actually exists on the server.

◆ In our example, there's just one attribute, `content`. We've specified that the content of the file should be `Hello, world`. If the file is empty, or contains something else, Puppet will overwrite the file with what the manifest says it should contain.

◆ In this case, the file will be empty the first time you apply the manifest, so Puppet will write the string `Hello, world` into it.

To check the results, run the following command:

```
ubuntu@demo:~$ cat /tmp/hello
Hello, world
```

Modifying existing files

What happens if the file already exists when Puppet runs, and it contains something else? Will Puppet change it?

```
ubuntu@demo:~$ echo Goodbye, world >/tmp/hello

ubuntu@demo:~$ puppet apply site.pp

Notice:/Stage[main]//File[/tmp/hello]/content: content
changed '{md5}cb2e4f7a21c01004462dd0a5ed9bd02a' to '{md5}
a7966bf58e23583c9a5a4059383ff850'

Notice: Finished catalog run in 0.04 seconds

ubuntu@demo:~$ cat /tmp/hello

Hello, world
```

The answer is yes. If any attribute of the file, including its contents, doesn't match the manifest, Puppet will change it so that it does.

This can lead to some surprising results if you manually edit a file managed by Puppet. If you make changes to a file without also changing the Puppet manifest to match, Puppet will overwrite the file the next time it runs, and your changes will be lost.

So it's a good idea to add a comment to files that Puppet is managing; something like:

```
# This file is managed by Puppet - any manual edits will be lost
```

Add this to Puppet's copy of the file when you first deploy it, and it will remind you and others not to make manual changes.

Exercise

Modify your manifest to have Puppet write a message to the system's /etc/motd file. It should be a cheerful, encouraging message so that users logging on to the system will feel that Puppet has things under control.

Organizing your manifests

So far your manifest for this machine is contained in a single file, but we're going to expand on that. Before things get more complicated, it's a good idea to set up a directory layout to keep files organized, like any source code.

Time for action – creating a directory structure

1. The top-level directory for Puppet manifests is usually named `puppet`, so first of all create this in your home directory:

   ```
   ubuntu@demo:~$ cd /home/ubuntu
   ubuntu@demo:~$ mkdir puppet
   ```

2. Within this directory, create a subdirectory named `manifests`:

   ```
   ubuntu@demo:~$ cd puppet
   ubuntu@demo:~/puppet$ mkdir manifests
   ```

3. Move your existing `site.pp` file into the `manifests` subdirectory:

   ```
   ubuntu@demo:~/puppet$ mv ../site.pp manifests/
   ```

4. Check that everything still works:

   ```
   ubuntu@demo:~/puppet$ puppet apply manifests/site.pp
   Notice: Finished catalog run in 0.03 seconds
   ```

   Your directory structure should now look as shown in the following diagram:

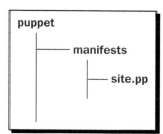

Creating a nodes.pp file

So far we've only dealt with one server, the demo server. But of course Puppet can manage many machines, each with different configurations, so we need a way to tell Puppet which configuration belongs to each machine.

This is done with a **node declaration** ("node" is the Puppet term for an individual machine that has a Puppet configuration). A node declaration looks like this:

```
node NODENAME {
    RESOURCE
    RESOURCE
    ...
}
```

Here NODENAME is the hostname of the relevant machine, and RESOURCE is a resource declaration.

If resources are not contained inside a node declaration, Puppet will always apply them (as we saw with the /tmp/hello file). But if they are inside a node declaration, Puppet will apply them only on a machine whose hostname matches the node name.

You could put all your Puppet manifests in a single file, and it would make no difference to Puppet. But it's much better and easier to manage if you break them up into several files. Conventionally, the top-level "master" file that includes everything else is named site.pp. You should put your node declarations in a file named nodes.pp, and we'll do this in the next example.

Time for action – creating a node declaration

Let's reorganize the manifest to move the /tmp/hello file within a node declaration for the demo server.

1. Create the file manifests/nodes.pp with the following contents:

```
node 'demo' {
  file { '/tmp/hello':
    content => "Hello, world\n",
  }
}
```

2. Change the manifests/site.pp file so it contains:

```
import 'nodes.pp'
```

3. Your puppet directory should now look as shown in the following diagram:

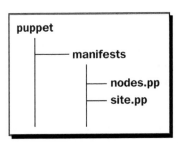

4. Check whether everything still works:

```
ubuntu@demo:~/puppet$ puppet apply manifests/site.pp
Notice: Finished catalog run in 0.03 seconds
```

What just happened?

When you run `puppet` apply, Puppet looks at the hostname of the machine (`demo` in this case) and tries to find a node declaration that matches it. It finds one:

```
node 'demo' {
  file { '/tmp/hello':
    content => "Hello, world\n",
  }
}
```

So it will apply everything within the `node 'demo'` declaration, which in our example has already been applied, so there's nothing for Puppet to do for now.

Although Puppet doesn't really mind how you organize your manifests within files—you can have everything within one big `site.pp` file if you like—it's a good idea to split them up into logical divisions. A common practice is to keep `site.pp` fairly small and just use it to load other manifest files, such as `nodes.pp`.

Summary

A quick rundown of what we've learned in this chapter.

Installing Puppet

You can install Puppet by downloading and installing the Puppet Labs APT repo package, then running `apt-get install` **puppet**.

Manifests

A **manifest** consists of a list of **resource declarations**. A resource declaration specifies a particular aspect of system configuration that you want Puppet to manage: a file, for example.

Resource declarations consist of a **name** and a list of **attributes**. The resource name is a unique identifier, which you can use to refer to this specific resource, if you need to. Its attributes specify various things about the resource that you want to control with Puppet.

Different types of resources have different attributes, but for a `file` resource, attributes include `content`, which specifies the contents of the file as a string.

Puppet processes a manifest by comparing the specified resources to what currently exists on the machine. Any missing resources will be created; attributes that do not match will be changed to match the manifest.

Manual changes to a file managed by Puppet will be lost when Puppet next applies the manifest.

Nodes

Node declarations identify a specific machine by its hostname, and tell Puppet which resources should be applied to that node. Any resources that are not part of a node declaration will be applied to all nodes. Put your node declarations in nodes.pp.

3

Packages, Files, and Services

It's not denial. I'm just selective about the reality I accept.

– Bill Watterson, "Calvin & Hobbes"

The most common types of resources you'll manage with Puppet are packages, files, and services. They often occur together, with a package providing a service, and the service requiring a configuration file. In this chapter you'll see how to use Puppet to manage these resources effectively.

Packages

Puppet's package resource will install, update, or remove a package for you, using the system native package management tools (in the case of Ubuntu, that's the **Advanced Package Tool (APT)**. If you were setting up a server manually, you might run a command such as:

```
apt-get install nginx
```

With Puppet, you can give a resource declaration such as:

```
package { 'nginx':
  ensure => installed,
}
```

Puppet will take the necessary actions by running `apt-get` behind the scenes.

Time for action – installing Nginx

Your mission for today is to use Puppet to install the Nginx web server and deploy a holding page for the `cat-pictures.com` website. Let's start by recalling what your Puppet directory structure should look like, as shown in the following diagram:

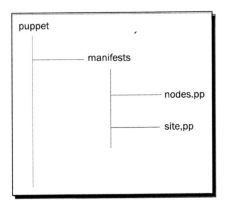

1. Edit the `nodes.pp` file so it looks like this:

    ```
    node 'demo' {
      package { 'nginx':
        ensure => installed,
      }
    }
    ```

    Replace `demo` with the hostname of the machine you're using.

2. Run Puppet:

```
ubuntu@demo:~/puppet$ sudo puppet apply manifests/site.pp
Notice: /Stage[main]//Node[demo]/Package[nginx]/ensure: ensure
changed 'purged' to 'present'
Notice: Finished catalog run in 3.10 seconds
```

What just happened?

Let's look at the preceding code in detail:

```
node 'demo' {
  ...
}
```

Remember that the node keyword introduces a node declaration, a list of resources that are to be applied only to node demo.

```
package { 'nginx':
  ensure => installed,
}
```

In this case, there is one resource, of type package. As with the file resource we created in *Chapter 2, First steps with Puppet*, the resource declaration consists of the following:

- ◆ The type of resource: package
- ◆ The name of the instance: nginx
- ◆ A list of attributes

Each resource type has a different list of attributes that you can control. A useful attribute for package resources is ensure. We use this attribute to install (or sometimes remove) packages.

```
ensure => installed,
```

When we apply this manifest, Puppet checks whether the nginx package is installed. If this is the first time you've applied the manifest, the package probably won't be present, so Puppet prints a message telling us that the package is being installed:

```
Notice: /Stage[main]//Node[demo]/Package[nginx]/ensure: ensure changed
'purged' to 'present'
```

As we saw with the file resource, once the resource has been created the first time, subsequent Puppet runs will do nothing because the state of the system already matches the manifest:

```
ubuntu@demo:~/puppet$ sudo puppet apply manifests/site.pp
Notice: Finished catalog run in 0.08 seconds
```

More about packages

We've seen how to use the `package` resource to install packages, but it has a few other tricks.

Installing specific versions

If you specify `ensure => installed` for a package, Puppet will install whatever is the current version of the package available from the repository at the time. This can cause differences between machines that are built at different times. Say you build `webserver1` on Monday, and on Tuesday morning a new version of Nginx is released upstream and pushed to the Ubuntu repositories. When you build `webserver2` on Tuesday afternoon, it will pick up a different version of Nginx than `webserver1`. So the machines end up with different configurations.

We'd prefer that our servers all be in the same state. To make sure this is the case, you can specify a version identifier for the package instead of `installed`:

```
package { 'nginx':
  ensure => '1.1.19-1ubuntu0.1',
}
```

The exact version string will depend on the Linux distribution and package repository you're using. To see what version of a package you currently have installed on Ubuntu, you can run the following command:

```
ubuntu@demo:~/puppet$ apt-cache policy nginx

nginx:
  Installed: 1.1.19-1ubuntu0.1
  Candidate: 1.1.19-1ubuntu0.1
  Version table:
 *** 1.1.19-1ubuntu0.1 0
        500 http://us-east-1.ec2.archive.ubuntu.com/ubuntu/ precise-
updates/universe amd64 Packages
        100 /var/lib/dpkg/status
     1.1.19-1 0
        500 http://us-east-1.ec2.archive.ubuntu.com/ubuntu/ precise/
universe amd64 Packages
```

What if package names are different on different operating systems? This does happen; for example, the package that manages NTP may be called `ntp` on some distributions and `ntpd` on others. If you have to write Puppet code that takes account of platform differences like this, you can use a Puppet construct called a **selector** to choose the appropriate package name. This is explained in detail later in the book, in *Chapter 8, Expressions and Logic*.

Removing packages

Occasionally you need to make sure a package is removed entirely from a machine, perhaps because it could cause conflicts with a package you're installing. If you're using the Nginx web server, for example, it's a good idea to remove the Apache package that ships with Ubuntu by default. If Apache is running, Nginx can't start, because Apache will grab the web server port.

```
package { 'apache2.2-common':
  ensure => absent,
}
```

Using `ensure => absent` will remove the package if it's installed.

Updating packages

Another value that `ensure` can take on a `package` resource is `latest`. This will cause Puppet to check which version of the package is available in the repository (if you're using Ubuntu, this includes any additional APT sources that you may have configured, such as the Puppet Labs repo). If it is newer than the installed version, Puppet will upgrade the package to the latest version.

```
package { 'puppet':
  ensure => latest,
}
```

Just because you *can* do this doesn't mean it's necessarily a good idea. Upgrading a package version can cause unexpected failures or problems, so I tend to avoid doing this on production systems. I certainly don't want it happening automatically, in the middle of the night, when I'm not around to respond to any issues.

If you run a staging server on which you can test any updates or changes before applying them to production (an approach I heartily endorse), this can be a good way to do it. You can have your staging server `ensure => latest` for critical packages and thus find out straight away if a new upstream package release breaks your system.

Also, `ensure => latest` can be a good way of managing updates if you control the package repository (for example, if you run your own APT repo. You can find a recipe to do this in *Chapter 5, Working with Files and Packages* of *The Puppet Cookbook*, Packt Publishing). In this situation, you only release a package to your repository once you have tested it thoroughly and verified that it doesn't cause any problems. Once it's available in the repo, all machines will update their versions automatically using `ensure => latest`.

Modules

To make your Puppet manifests more readable and maintainable, it's a good idea to arrange them into **modules**. A Puppet module is a way of grouping related resources. In our example, we're going to make an `nginx` module that will contain all Puppet code relating to Nginx.

Time for action – creating an Nginx module

1. In your `puppet` directory, create the following subdirectories:

```
ubuntu@demo:~/puppet$ mkdir modules
ubuntu@demo:~/puppet$ mkdir modules/nginx
ubuntu@demo:~/puppet$ mkdir modules/nginx/manifests
```

2. Create the file `modules/nginx/manifests/init.pp` with the following contents:

```
# Manage nginx webserver
class nginx {
  package { 'nginx':
    ensure => installed,
  }
}
```

3. Edit the `manifests/nodes.pp` file as follows:

```
node 'demo' {
  include nginx
}
```

4. Run Puppet to make sure everything is correct. There should be no changes:

```
ubuntu@demo:~/puppet$ sudo puppet apply manifests/site.pp
--modulepath=/home/ubuntu/puppet/modules/
Notice: Finished catalog run in 0.08 seconds
```

Your directory structure should now look like this:

```
puppet
            manifests
                        nodes.pp
                        site.pp
            modules
                nginx
                    manifests
                        init.pp
```

What just happened?

We've reorganized the code without changing what it actually does (a process called **refactoring**). Before the refactoring, our node declaration looked like this:

```
node 'demo' {
  package { 'nginx':
    ensure => installed,
  }
}
```

Now the node declaration looks like this:

```
node 'demo' {
  include nginx
}
```

You can see that the nginx resource has been replaced by the line include nginx. To Puppet, this means, "Look for a **class** called nginx and include all the resources in it on this node."

A class in Puppet is simply a named bundle of resources that you want to apply together. A module might contain many classes, but our example nginx module just contains one class, also named nginx:

```
class nginx {
  package { 'nginx':
    ensure => installed,
  }
}
```

The class keyword declares a group of resources (here, the package resource for Nginx) identified by the name nginx. We can then use the include keyword elsewhere to include all the resources in the class at once.

Why do this? Well, for one thing, it means we could include the `nginx` class on many nodes without repeating the same resource declarations over and over:

```
node 'demo' {
  include nginx
}

node 'demo2' {
  include nginx
}

node 'demo3' {
  include nginx
}
```

But we're getting ahead of ourselves. For now, let's just say that grouping resources into classes and modules helps us organize our code so it's easy to read and maintain.

Did you notice we used a slightly different form of the `puppet apply` command?

puppet apply manifests/site.pp --modulepath=/home/ubuntu/puppet/modules/

We haven't needed to give a `modulepath` argument before, but now we're using a module, so we need to tell Puppet where to find it.

Time for action – making a "puppet apply" command

You'll be running `puppet apply` pretty often, so to save typing I suggest you make a little script to wrap this command up with all the arguments you need.

1. Create the file `/usr/local/bin/papply` using the following command:

   `ubuntu@demo:~/puppet$ sudo vi /usr/local/bin/papply`

2. Add the following contents (the `sudo puppet apply...` command should all be on one line):

   ```
   #!/bin/sh
   sudo puppet apply /home/ubuntu/puppet/manifests/site.pp
   --modulepath=/home/ubuntu/puppet/modules/ $*
   ```

3. Set execute permissions on this file:

   `ubuntu@demo:~/puppet$ sudo chmod a+x /usr/local/bin/papply`

   Now whenever you need to run Puppet, you can simply run:

   `ubuntu@demo:~/puppet$ papply`

Services

So we're using a module to manage Nginx on the server. That's great, but so far we've only installed the `nginx` package. In order to run the web server, we would need to start and stop it manually using the command line. Fortunately, we can automate this with Puppet as well.

Time for action – adding the Nginx service

1. Edit the `modules/nginx/manifests/init.pp` file as follows:

    ```
    # Manage nginx webserver
    class nginx {
      package { 'apache2.2-common':
        ensure => absent,
      }

      package { 'nginx':
        ensure => installed,
        require => Package['apache2.2-common'],
      }

      service { 'nginx':
        ensure  => running,
        require => Package['nginx'],
      }
    }
    ```

2. Run Puppet as follows:

    ```
    ubuntu@demo:~/puppet$ papply

    Notice: /Stage[main]/Nginx/Package[apache2.2-common]/ensure:
    removed

    Notice: /Stage[main]/Nginx/Service[nginx]/ensure: ensure changed
    'stopped' to 'running'

    Notice: Finished catalog run in 0.47 seconds
    ```

What just happened?

Let's look at the code you added in detail:

```
package { 'apache2.2-common':
  ensure => absent,
}
```

On Ubuntu, the default setup includes the Apache web server, which would conflict with Nginx if we tried to run it at the same time. So by specifying `ensure => absent`, we remove the Apache package.

The next section declares the `nginx` package:

```
package { 'nginx':
  ensure => installed,
  require => Package['apache2.2-common'],
}
```

The `require` attribute tells Puppet that this resource depends on another resource, which must be applied first. In this case, we want the removal of Apache to be applied before the installation of Nginx. We'll see more about the `require` attribute in the *Requiring resources* section.

> Is there any implied order to attributes? In other words, does Puppet do the `ensure` part before the `require` part, or doesn't it matter what order you list them in? Actually, it doesn't matter; Puppet will consider all the attributes of a resource before making any changes, so you can think of them as all being applied at the same time. If a resource uses `ensure`, it's good style to put that first, but it doesn't make any difference to Puppet.

Next, we declare the `nginx` service:

```
service { 'nginx':
  ensure  => running,
  require => Package['nginx'],
}
```

By now you know that this declares a resource of type `service`. Service resources manage **daemons**, or background processes, on the server. The `ensure` attribute tells Puppet what state the service should be in:

```
ensure  => running,
```

When you ran Puppet, it checked the status of the `nginx` service and found it stopped, so Puppet started the service for you:

```
Notice: /Stage[main]/Nginx/Service[nginx]/ensure: ensure changed
'stopped' to 'running'
```

If you ran Puppet again, there would be no change because Nginx is already running, so the server matches the manifest.

On Ubuntu, packages that provide a service (such as Nginx) are often configured to start the service automatically when they're installed. However, we make this explicit in Puppet by saying the following:

```
ensure  => running,
```

On other operating systems, services may not be set up to auto-start when installed, and in any case we want to have Puppet ensure that the service is always running. If it gets stopped for any reason, Puppet will restart it when the manifest is applied.

Requiring resources

What about that `require` attribute? `require` specifies a dependency between resources. For example, we have to have the Nginx package installed before we can run the Nginx service. That makes sense, and the `require` attribute expresses this relationship between the two resources.

```
require => Package['nginx'],
```

Any resource can have a `require` attribute, and the value must be another resource declared somewhere in your manifest.

Did you notice that `Package` is capitalized? That tells Puppet you're referring to a named instance of a package resource, with the name following in square brackets:

```
Package['nginx']
```

You might wonder what happens if your resources `require` each other in a loop: one resource requires another, which requires another, which requires the first resource, similar to this:

```
file { '/tmp/file1':
  require => File['/tmp/file2'],
}
file { '/tmp/file2':
  require => File['/tmp/file3'],
}
file { '/tmp/file3':
  require => File['/tmp/file1'],
}
```

Will Puppet just go round and round in circles forever? Let's see:

```
ubuntu@demo:~/puppet$ papply
Error: Could not apply complete catalog: Found 1 dependency cycle:
(File[/tmp/file1] => File[/tmp/file3] => File[/tmp/file2] => File[/tmp/
file1])
Try the '--graph' option and opening the resulting '.dot' file in
OmniGraffle or GraphViz
```

Sometimes dependency cycles can be more subtle than this, and harder to figure out. As the error message suggests, you can get some help by giving the --graph option to Puppet, which will then produce a diagram of the dependency cycle for you.

Note that Puppet can only figure out explicit dependency cycles, as in this example. More problematic are cycles caused by side effects; if a file notifies a service, and the service itself causes the file to change, Puppet will detect that the file has changed and so notify the service, and this will continue forever. Happily, this situation doesn't arise very often, but it can be hard to work out what's going on when it does.

More about services

Puppet's service resource has a few other facilities, depending on the underlying operating system and what it supports. Here are some of the features you are most likely to use (and that are supported on Ubuntu).

Starting a service at boot time

Puppet can control whether a service starts during the system boot process, using the enable attribute:

```
service { 'nginx':
  ensure => running,
  enable => true,
}
```

Setting enable => true will configure the service to start at boot time (specifically, on Ubuntu, to start in runlevels 2, 3, 4, and 5, and stop in runlevels 0, 1, and 6). To disable the automatic service startup (for example, if the service is managed by a high-availability framework such as Heartbeat), set enable => false.

Services that don't support "status"

Most `init` and `upstart` (service management) scripts on Ubuntu support the `start` and `stop` commands; for example:

```
ubuntu@demo:~/puppet$ sudo service nginx stop
Stopping nginx: nginx.
ubuntu@demo:~/puppet$ sudo service nginx start
Starting nginx: nginx.
```

Some also support a `status` command, which determines whether or not the service is currently running:

```
ubuntu@demo:~/puppet$ sudo service nginx status
 * nginx is running
```

When Puppet manages a service, it will try to use the `status` command to check the service's status. In some cases this doesn't work, either because the script doesn't support the `status` argument or because it returns an incorrect exit code. If you have this problem, you can use the `hasstatus` attribute to change this behavior:

```
service { 'my-service':
  ensure    => running,
  hasstatus => false,
}
```

If `hasstatus` is false for a service, Puppet will instead look at the system process list (such as that produced by the `ps` command) and see if the service name is listed in it. If it is, Puppet assumes the service is running. Otherwise, it will attempt to start it.

If the service name itself wouldn't appear in the process list, you can specify a different pattern for Puppet to search for using the `pattern` attribute:

```
service { 'my-service':
  ensure    => running,
  hasstatus => false,
  pattern   => 'ruby myservice.rb',
}
```

If the service status can't be detected from the process list, you can give Puppet a command to run that will return an appropriate exit status (0 for running, any other value for not running) using the `status` attribute:

```
service { 'my-service':
  ensure    => running,
  hasstatus => false,
  status    => 'grep running /var/lib/myservice/status.txt',
}
```

Specifying how to start, stop, or restart a service

Sometimes Puppet needs to restart the service (for example, if its config file changes and you are using `notify` to tell the service about it). By default Puppet will stop the service, then start it.

However, some services support a `restart` or `reload` command, which may be preferable to stopping and starting the service. For example, some daemons keep a lot of state information in memory, and if you stopped the service this would be lost.

In this case, you can specify a command that Puppet should use to restart the service using the `restart` attribute:

```
service { 'ssh':
  ensure  => running,
  restart => '/usr/sbin/service ssh reload',
}
```

If you need to, you can also provide a `start` or `stop` attribute, specifying commands to start or stop the service. This isn't usually necessary, but it's there just in case.

Files

So Nginx is installed and running, but it's not yet serving a website. To do that, we have to have Puppet install a config file on the server to define an Nginx **virtual host**. This will tell Nginx how to respond to requests for the `cat-pictures` website.

Time for action – deploying a virtual host

First, we'll create a simple website for Nginx to serve.

1. Create the directory `/var/www/cat-pictures`:

   ```
   ubuntu@demo:~/puppet$ sudo mkdir -p /var/www/cat-pictures
   ```

2. Add a small HTML file:

   ```
   ubuntu@demo:~/puppet$ sudo su -c 'echo "I can haz cat pictures?"
   >/var/www/cat-pictures/index.html'
   ```

   Next, we'll create the virtual host file for Puppet to deploy:

3. Create the directory `modules/nginx/files`:

   ```
   ubuntu@demo:~/puppet$ mkdir modules/nginx/files
   ```

4. Create the file `modules/nginx/files/cat-pictures.conf` with the following contents:

```
server {
  listen 80;
  root /var/www/cat-pictures;
  server_name cat-pictures.com;
}
```

Next, we'll add a resource that will deploy this file to the server.

5. Edit the file `modules/nginx/manifests/init.pp` so it looks like this:

```
# Manage nginx webserver
class nginx {
  package { 'nginx':
    ensure => installed,
  }

  service { 'nginx':
    ensure  => running,
    require => Package['nginx'],
  }

  file { '/etc/nginx/sites-enabled/default':
    source => 'puppet:///modules/nginx/cat-pictures.conf',
    notify => Service['nginx'],
  }
}
```

Be careful with the `source` value in the code above. It starts with `puppet` followed by three slashes, not two:

```
puppet:///modules/nginx...
```

Not

```
puppet://modules/nginx...
```

6. Run Puppet:

```
ubuntu@demo:~/puppet$ papply
```

```
Notice: /Stage[main]/Nginx/File[/etc/nginx/sites-enabled/default]/
ensure: defined content as '{md5}0750fd1b8da76b84f2597de76c1b9bce'
```

```
Notice: /Stage[main]/Nginx/Service[nginx]: Triggered 'refresh'
from 1 events
```

```
Notice: Finished catalog run in 0.36 seconds
```

7. Finally, to make sure everything worked properly, request the website:

```
ubuntu@demo:~/puppet$ curl localhost
I can haz cat pictures?
```

What just happened?

Here's the new Puppet code we added:

```
file { '/etc/nginx/sites-enabled/default':
  source => 'puppet:///modules/nginx/cat-pictures.conf',
  notify => Service['nginx'],
}
```

Again, we'll go through it line by line.

```
file { '/etc/nginx/sites-enabled/default':
```

We're declaring a `file` resource with the path `/etc/nginx/sites-enabled/default`.

```
source => 'puppet:///modules/nginx/cat-pictures.conf',
```

`source` is a file attribute that we haven't seen before. Previously we used `content` to supply the contents of the file as a string. Here, `source` tells Puppet where to find a copy of the file:

```
puppet:///modules/nginx/cat-pictures.conf
```

This looks a bit like a URL, but it tells Puppet to look in the `modules/nginx/files` directory for a file named `cat-pictures.conf`.

 Notice that the source URL doesn't contain the word `files`. It's just `puppet:///modules/MODULENAME/FILENAME`. When Puppet translates this URL into a disk path, it becomes `modules/MODULENAME/files/FILENAME`. If you find this confusing, you're in good company.

One question that might occur to you is, "What about when I'm running Puppet on several different machines? Where does the file come from in that case? Will each machine have its own copy of the file, or will it come from some central place?"

The answer depends on how you run Puppet across multiple machines; whether you use a central server (known as a **Puppetmaster**) or whether each machine gets its own copy of the manifest. We'll explore this in detail later, and build a complete working solution, in *Chapter 4, Managing Puppet with Git*.

Notifying other resources

`notify` is another attribute that we haven't seen before:

```
notify => Service['nginx'],
```

It means "whenever this file is changed, tell `Service['nginx']` to restart". That's what we saw happen as Puppet deployed the file (which of course counts as a change):

Notice: /Stage[main]/Nginx/File[/etc/nginx/sites-enabled/default]/ensure: defined content as '{md5}0750fd1b8da76b84f2597de76c1b9bce'

Notice:/Stage[main]/Nginx/Service[nginx]: Triggered 'refresh' from 1 events

> When a `file` resource notifies a `service` resource, the file must be present before the service is started. So if a file notifies a service, it's just another way of saying that the service requires the file. You can express the relationship either way, and the result will be the same.

The package–file–service pattern

The pattern you've just learnt is a very useful one. It'll cover most services that you need to automate.

```
class THE_STUFF {
  package { THE_STUFF:
    ensure => installed,
  }

  service { THE_STUFF:
    ensure  => running,
    require => Package[THE_STUFF],
  }

  file { '/etc/THE_STUFF.conf':
    source => 'puppet:///modules/THE_STUFF/THE_STUFF.conf',
    notify => Service[THE_STUFF],
  }
}
```

In English, this says:

- The service `THE_STUFF` should be running
- Before the service `THE_STUFF` is started, the package `THE_STUFF` should be installed
- Before the service `THE_STUFF` is started, the file `/etc/THE_STUFF.conf` should be present (remember that "A notifies B" implies "B requires A")
- If the file `/etc/THE_STUFF.conf` changes, restart the service `THE_STUFF`

Exercise

Modify the `nginx` class to create `/var/www/cat-pictures` and the `index.html` file you previously set up manually.

Summary

A quick rundown of what we've learnt in this chapter.

Packages

The `package` resource is used to manage packages. To install a package, you set the `ensure` attribute to `installed`.

To remove the package, use `ensure => absent`.

To install a specific version `VERSION`, use `ensure => VERSION`.

To install the latest version of the package available in the repo, use `ensure => latest`.

Modules

To help organize your code, you can put related resources into a module. For example, to create an `nginx` module, create the file `modules/nginx/manifests/init.pp` and put this in it:

```
# Manage nginx webserver
class nginx {
  ...
}
```

To apply this to a node, use:

```
include nginx
```

Services

To manage services, use the `service` resource type. The `ensure` attribute controls whether or not the service should be running. To specify that the service should be running, use `ensure => running`. To specify that it should be stopped, use `ensure => stopped`.

Starting services at boot

The `enable` attribute controls whether or not a service is started at boot time. To start the service at boot time, use `enable => true`. If you don't want it to start on boot (unlikely, but possible) use `enable => false`.

Service status options

Puppet will use the service's own control script to determine whether the service is running, by calling `service SERVICENAME status` (at least on UNIX-like systems).

If a service's control script doesn't support a `status` command, you can set `hasstatus => false` for the service resource. In this case, Puppet will look in the system process table to see if the service is running.

If you need Puppet to search the process table for something other than the service's name, you can specify what to search for using the `pattern` attribute.

If searching the process table won't work, you can provide a command for Puppet to use to determine the service's status, using the `status` attribute.

Service control commands

If you want to restart a service some other way than just stopping and starting the service, you can give Puppet the command you want to use via the `restart` attribute.

You can also specify custom service start and stop commands using the `start` and `stop` attributes.

Resource dependencies

You can specify a dependency between resources using the `require` attribute:

```
require => Package['nginx'],
```

If resource B requires resource A, then Puppet will make sure the resources are applied in the right order.

Files

You can have Puppet deploy a copy of a file using the `source` attribute:

```
file { '/etc/nginx/sites-enabled/default':
  source => 'puppet:///modules/nginx/cat-pictures.conf',
}
```

File resources can trigger a service to be restarted using the `notify` attribute. This is useful for configuration files, for which changes often don't take effect until the relevant service is restarted:

```
notify => Service['nginx'],
```

4
Managing Puppet with Git

If you do not change direction, you may end up where you are heading.

– Lao-tzu

In this chapter you'll learn how to use the Git version control system to manage your Puppet manifests. I'll also show you how to use Git to distribute the manifests to multiple machines, so that you can start managing your whole network with Puppet.

If you're already familiar with Git, you can save some reading by skipping ahead to the *Time for action – importing your manifests into Git* section. If not, here's a gentle introduction.

What is version control?

If you haven't used Git, or a similar version control tool (CVS and Subversion are some other examples), you might be wondering what it is and why we should use it. To explain this, let's look back to one of the system administration problems we talked about in *Chapter 1, Introduction to Puppet*: the problem of tracking code changes.

Even if you're the only person who works on a piece of source code (for example, Puppet manifests), it's still useful to be able to see what changes you made, and when. For example, you might remember that you fixed a bug last week, but not exactly how, and it would be handy to be able to see exactly what lines in which file were changed.

When you're working on code with others, you need a way to communicate changes to the rest of the team. A version control tool such as Git not only tracks everyone's changes, but lets you record a message about what you did and why. For example, a change might be marked with the following message:

```
Author: John Arundel <john@bitfieldconsulting.com>

Date:    Wed Aug 8 18:57:25 2012 +0100


    Increase conntrack table size on proxy servers (fixes issue #110)
```

It tells you when the change happened, who made it, and (if the commit message is well written) why it was made. You can also see what file was changed, and which lines were added, altered, or removed as follows:

```
modules/proxy/files/sysctl.conf
+net.ipv4.netfilter.ip_conntrack_max = 256000
```

Imagine you're trying to track down a bug; having a complete history of code changes would be a big help. It also means you can, if necessary, roll back the state of the code to any point in history and examine it.

You might think this introduces a lot of extra complications. In fact, it's very simple. Git keeps out of your way until you need it, and all you have to do is write a commit message when you decide to record changes to the code.

Another very important role of version control is to allow several people to work independently on the code, and to merge all their separate changes back together and resolve any conflicts. Git provides very powerful tools for doing this. If you're working on Puppet code in a team, it's critical that you use some kind of version control to handle it.

In this chapter we'll add Git version control to the manifests we've been developing, and I'll show you some of the useful things Git can do.

Time for action – importing your manifests into Git

1. Run the following command:

   ```
   ubuntu@demo:~$ sudo apt-get install git
   ```

2. Check if Git is correctly installed (the exact version number doesn't matter, as long as it's reasonably up-to-date):

   ```
   ubuntu@demo:~$ git --version
   git version 1.7.9.5
   ```

3. Now initialize Git in your /home/ubuntu/puppet directory:

   ```
   ubuntu@demo:~$ cd puppet
   ubuntu@demo:~/puppet$ git init
   Initialized empty Git repository in /home/ubuntu/puppet/.git/
   ```

4. Now set your identification details for Git (use your own name and e-mail):

   ```
   ubuntu@demo:~/puppet$ git config --global user.name "John Arundel"
   ubuntu@demo:~/puppet$ git config --global user.email john@
   bitfieldconsulting.com
   ```

5. Tell Git to manage all the files and subdirectories in this directory:

   ```
   ubuntu@demo:~/puppet$ git add .
   ```

6. Finally, have Git take a snapshot of the current state of the code:

   ```
   ubuntu@demo:~/puppet$ git commit -m "importing"
   [master (root-commit) 36f88cb] importing
    4 files changed, 25 insertions(+)
    create mode 100644 manifests/nodes.pp
    create mode 100644 manifests/site.pp
    create mode 100644 modules/nginx/files/cat-pictures.conf
    create mode 100644 modules/nginx/manifests/init.pp
   ```

What just happened?

Git tracks changes to a particular set of files. The changes are stored in Git's database, known as a **repository** ("repo" for short). When you run the git init command, it tells Git to create a new repository in the current directory.

When you create a new repo, it contains no files, so the git add command adds files to the list that Git should track:

```
git add .
```

This command adds everything in this directory. The full stop (.) is UNIX shorthand for the current directory.

Instead of storing every successive version of a file, Git just keeps the differences. For example, if you add a line to a file and then commit that change, Git stores only the new line and the details of which file it modifies.

For this to work, of course, there has to be an initial commit; a snapshot of the starting state that Git will then track changes from. This first commit is what you created when you ran the following command:

```
git commit -m "Importing"
```

The -m switch lets you attach a message to the commit, so that you or other people can see your comments in the history.

Time for action – committing and inspecting changes

Let's make a change to the manifest and then use Git to see some information about it.

1. Edit the file modules/nginx/manifests/init.pp and find the section defining the nginx service:

    ```
    service { 'nginx':
      ensure  => running,
      require => Package['nginx'],
    }
    ```

2. Add the following line:

    ```
    service { 'nginx':
      ensure  => running,
      enable  => true,
      require => Package['nginx'],
    }
    ```

3. Save the file and run the following command:

    ```
    ubuntu@demo:~/puppet$ git status
    # On branch master
    # Changes not staged for commit:
    #   (use "git add <file>..." to update what will be committed)
    #   (use "git checkout -- <file>..." to discard changes in working
    directory)
    #
    #       modified:   modules/nginx/manifests/init.pp
    ```

```
#
no changes added to commit (use "git add" and/or "git commit -a")
```

4. Use `git diff` to show you how the code differs from the snapshot taken at the last commit:

```
ubuntu@demo:~/puppet$ git diff
diff --git a/modules/nginx/manifests/init.pp b/modules/nginx/
manifests/init.pp
index b152f17..f272a7c 100644
--- a/modules/nginx/manifests/init.pp
+++ b/modules/nginx/manifests/init.pp
@@ -5,6 +5,7 @@ class nginx {

    service { 'nginx':
      ensure  => running,
+     enable  => true,
      require => Package['nginx'],
    }
```

5. Add the changed file to the set that will be included in the next commit:

```
ubuntu@demo:~/puppet$ git add modules/nginx/manifests/init.pp
```

6. Commit the change:

```
ubuntu@demo:~/puppet$ git commit -m "Have nginx start at boot
time"
[master ad71988] have nginx start at boot time
 1 file changed, 1 insertion(+)
```

7. Check the log of changes:

```
ubuntu@demo:~/puppet$ git log
commit ad719887ef68535dd6b76bab8bcee9b76edb3c98
Author: John Arundel <john@bitfieldconsulting.com>
Date:   Mon Oct 22 17:08:34 2012 +0000

    Have nginx start at boot time

commit 36f88cbf36782bd8e74499bb23a3a8aa5cc44ef9
Author: John Arundel <john@bitfieldconsulting.com>
Date:   Mon Oct 22 16:38:58 2012 +0000

    Importing
```

8. Use `git whatchanged` to have Git display a `diff` showing what was changed in the commit:

```
ubuntu@demo:~/puppet$ git whatchanged -p -n 1
commit ad719887ef68535dd6b76bab8bcee9b76edb3c98
Author: John Arundel <john@bitfieldconsulting.com>
Date:   Mon Oct 22 17:08:34 2012 +0000

    Have nginx start at boot time

diff --git a/modules/nginx/manifests/init.pp b/modules/nginx/
manifests/init.pp
index b152f17..f272a7c 100644
--- a/modules/nginx/manifests/init.pp
+++ b/modules/nginx/manifests/init.pp
@@ -5,6 +5,7 @@ class nginx {

   service { 'nginx':
     ensure  => running,
+    enable  => true,
     require => Package['nginx'],
   }
```

What just happened?

The line you added to `nginx.pp` is useful; it tells Puppet to configure the `nginx` service so that it starts when the machine boots.

```
    enable  => true,
```

You have now changed the code so that it differs from that stored in Git's database, and you can see which files are different using `git status`:

```
#       modified:   modules/nginx/manifests/init.pp
```

To see exactly what the differences are, use `git diff`:

```
   service { 'nginx':
     ensure  => running,
+    enable  => true,
     require => Package['nginx'],
   }
```

The + indicates a line was added.

The next step was to tell Git to include this change in the next commit, by using the `git add` command:

```
ubuntu@demo:~/puppet$ git add modules/nginx/manifests/init.pp
```

Now you make the actual commit, with a suitable explanatory message:

```
ubuntu@demo:~/puppet$ git commit -m "have nginx start at boot time"
```

The change (or more accurately, set of changes; in this case we only made one) is now stored in Git's database, and we can see it using the `git log` command:

```
ubuntu@demo:~/puppet$ git log
commit ad719887ef68535dd6b76bab8bcee9b76edb3c98
Author: John Arundel <john@bitfieldconsulting.com>
Date:   Mon Oct 22 17:08:34 2012 +0000

    Have nginx start at boot time

commit 36f88cbf36782bd8e74499bb23a3a8aa5cc44ef9
Author: John Arundel <john@bitfieldconsulting.com>
Date:   Mon Oct 22 16:38:58 2012 +0000

    Importing
```

The long string of hexadecimal characters following `commit` is called the **commit hash**, and it uniquely identifies the commit in this repo:

```
commit ad719887ef68535dd6b76bab8bcee9b76edb3c98
```

Whenever you need to refer to a particular commit, you can use this hash to identify it.

As time goes on, you will still be able to see every change you've committed to the repo right back to the initial import. The `git whatchanged` command shows you the effect of each change, just like `git diff` does for uncommitted changes:

```
    service { 'nginx':
        ensure  => running,
+       enable  => true,
        require => Package['nginx'],
    }
```

You can skip the `git add` step by using the `-a` flag to `git commit`, as follows:

`git commit -a -m "Have nginx start at boot time"`

This automatically adds all changed files to the commit. However, it's a good idea to use `git status` and `git add` to see precisely what changes you are committing. Sometimes you may want to split your changes into two or more separate commits.

Also, if you have added new files that Git doesn't know about yet, you'll still need to use `git add` to tell Git they should be placed under its control.

How often should I commit?

A common practice is to commit when the code is in a consistent, working state, and have the commit include a set of related changes made for some particular purpose. So, for example, if you are working to fix bug number 75 in your issue-tracking system, you might make changes to quite a few separate files and then, once you're happy the work is complete, make a single commit with a message such as:

`Make nginx restart more reliable (fixes issue #75)`

On the other hand, if you are making a large number of complicated changes and you are not sure quite when you'll be done, it might be wise to make a few separate commits along the way, so that if necessary you can roll the code back to a previous state. Commits cost nothing, so when you feel a commit is needed, go ahead and make it.

Branching

Git has a powerful feature called **branching**, which lets you create a parallel copy of the code (a branch) and make changes to it independently. At any time you can choose to merge those changes back into the master branch. Or, if changes have been made to the master branch in the meantime, you can merge those into your working branch and carry on.

This is extremely useful when working with Puppet, because it means you can switch a single machine to your branch while you're testing it and working on it. The changes you make won't be visible to other machines that aren't on your branch, so there's no danger of accidentally rolling out changes before you're ready.

Once you're done, you can merge your changes back into that master and have them roll out to all machines.

Similarly, two or more people can work independently on their own branches, exchanging individual commits with each other and with the master branch as they choose. This is a very flexible and useful way of working.

Distributing Puppet manifests

So far in this book we've only applied Puppet manifests to one server, using `puppet apply` with a local copy of the manifest. To manage several servers at once, we need to distribute the Puppet manifests to each machine so that they can be applied.

There are several ways to do this, and Puppet has a built-in server capability (Puppetmaster), which lets each client machine request its own compiled manifest via HTTP. However, when I work with clients to help them build Puppet infrastructures, I usually recommend a different approach, using Git to distribute the manifests.

This has a number of advantages over the Puppetmaster approach, and is in some ways simpler.

Reliability

Although your master Git server (or even GitHub) may go down, you will still be able to run Puppet on all your client machines and push changes to them using Git. Git is inherently distributed, unlike the Puppetmaster architecture.

Scalability

You can keep on adding machines indefinitely, and each one looks after itself. By contrast, using a Puppetmaster moves all the workload of compiling manifests from the client machine to a single server, which places heavy demands on that server as the network grows.

Simplicity

All you need to do is clone a Git repo. By contrast, adding new Puppet nodes using a Puppetmaster requires you to generate a certificate request on the client, and sign it on the server before Puppet can run. Automating this process adds complexity, and changing the Puppetmaster SSL certificate (for example, if the master server is replaced) requires resigning all the client certificates. You can set up autosigning, but this introduces a potentially quite serious security hole.

It's only fair to admit that there are different opinions about this, and some people favor the Puppetmaster approach, and even think it's simpler than using Git. However, what's simple to you depends on what you already know. Lots of people already know how to use Git; if not, it's a very useful thing to learn, and you can apply that knowledge to more than just Puppet.

In the following sections, we'll create a "master" repo, use it to distribute our manifests to a new server, and then set up an automatic method of pulling changes and applying them to each machine.

Time for action – creating a master Git repo

We're going to make a copy of our existing Puppet repo, which we can then clone on a new machine.

1. Create a directory to hold the repo:

```
ubuntu@demo:~/puppet$ sudo mkdir /var/git
```

2. Clone the repo, using the `--bare` flag:

```
ubuntu@demo:~/puppet$ cd /var/git
ubuntu@demo:/var/git$ sudo git clone --bare /home/ubuntu/puppet
Cloning into bare repository 'puppet.git'...
done.
```

3. Now create a `git` user that will own the master repo and control access to it:

```
ubuntu@demo:/var/git$ sudo useradd -d /var/git git
ubuntu@demo:/var/git$ sudo chown -R git:git /var/git
```

4. Just to verify that these steps have worked, check out a temporary clone of the master repo:

```
ubuntu@demo:/tmp$ cd /tmp
ubuntu@demo:/tmp$ git clone /var/git/puppet.git
Cloning into 'puppet'...
done.
ubuntu@demo:/tmp$ ls puppet
manifests   modules
ubuntu@demo:/tmp$ rm -r puppet
```

5. Now create a secure shell (SSH) keypair for the `git` user so that it can log in from remote machines to clone and update the Git repo. When prompted for a passphrase, just hit *Enter*.

```
ubuntu@demo:/tmp$ sudo su - git
$ ssh-keygen
Generating public/private rsa key pair.
Enter file in which to save the key (/var/git/.ssh/id_rsa):
Created directory '/var/git/.ssh'.
Enter passphrase (empty for no passphrase):
Enter same passphrase again:
Your identification has been saved in /var/git/.ssh/id_rsa.
Your public key has been saved in /var/git/.ssh/id_rsa.pub.
```

```
The key fingerprint is:
87:12:a4:3d:e3:da:79:01:19:d1:0b:1c:15:f8:7c:93 git@demo
The key's randomart image is:
+--[ RSA 2048]----+
|      .=*o.       |
|      ++o.        |
|    . B+ . .      |
|     . =+.E       |
|      o S...      |
|      o o o       |
|     . o .        |
|        .         |
|                  |
+-----------------+
```

The fingerprint and image will be different for your key, but that's fine.

6. Create an `authorized_keys` file for `git` containing the public key you just generated:

```
git@demo:~$ cd .ssh
git@demo:~/.ssh$ ls
git@demo:~/.ssh$ cp id_rsa.pub authorized_keys
```

7. You should now be able to log into the `git` account via SSH using this key:

```
git@demo:~/.ssh$ ssh git@localhost
Welcome to Ubuntu 12.04.1 LTS (GNU/Linux 3.2.0-29-virtual x86_64)
...
```

You now have a master Git repo containing your manifests, and an SSH key that you can use to check out the repo on other machines.

Time for action – cloning the repo to a new machine

You'll need a second machine similar to the one you have been using so far (either a cloud instance, a Vagrant VM, or a physical machine, whichever is convenient). Install Puppet and its dependencies as you did for the first machine in *Chapter 2, First steps with Puppet*, in the *Time for action – preparing for Puppet and Time for action – installing Puppet* sections.

1. Once the machine is set up, create the `git` user:

```
ubuntu@demo2:~$ sudo useradd -m git
```

2. Create a `.ssh` directory and private key file, and set appropriate permissions:

```
ubuntu@demo2:~$ sudo su - git
git@demo2:~$ mkdir .ssh
git@demo2:~$ chmod 700 .ssh
git@demo2:~$ touch .ssh/id_rsa
git@demo2:~$ chmod 600 .ssh/id_rsa
```

3. On your first server, display the SSH private key for `git` and copy it to the clipboard:

```
ubuntu@demo:~$ sudo cat ~git/.ssh/id_rsa
-----BEGIN RSA PRIVATE KEY-----
MIIEowIBAAKCAQEA1wR9i+bkwsNIcydlojhBH13ecuOhGfoJpjdjSjocBjf2fJRa
...
GOTLXyqpcrez/Ijbc9TJsaFNisnb1HqBR31J/N2StjHmwjtOmlwL
-----END RSA PRIVATE KEY-----
```

4. Now edit the private key file on the new server:

```
git@demo2:~$ vi .ssh/id_rsa
```

5. Press *i* to enter insert mode and paste the key from the clipboard:

```
-----BEGIN RSA PRIVATE KEY-----
MIIEowIBAAKCAQEA1wR9i+bkwsNIcydlojhBH13ecuOhGfoJpjdjSjocBjf2fJRa
...
GOTLXyqpcrez/Ijbc9TJsaFNisnb1HqBR31J/N2StjHmwjtOmlwL
-----END RSA PRIVATE KEY-----
```

6. Save the file and exit (`:wq`).

7. Test the private key by logging into the old server from the new (use the public IP address of your first server):

```
git@demo2:~$ ssh git@23.20.119.201
The authenticity of host '23.20.119.201 (23.20.119.201)' can't be
established.
ECDSA key fingerprint is 29:9d:2a:09:85:d1:2d:24:a2:e5:ff:0a:4a:75
:c2:6b.
Are you sure you want to continue connecting (yes/no)? yes
Warning: Permanently added '23.20.119.201' (ECDSA) to the list of
known hosts.
Welcome to Ubuntu 12.04.1 LTS (GNU/Linux 3.2.0-29-virtual x86_64)
```

8. You should now be able to clone the repo onto the new machine:

```
git@demo2:~$ git clone 23.20.119.201:/var/git/puppet.git
Cloning into 'puppet'...
remote: Counting objects: 17, done.
remote: Compressing objects: 100% (10/10), done.
remote: Total 17 (delta 1), reused 0 (delta 0)
Receiving objects: 100% (17/17), 1.27 KiB, done.
Resolving deltas: 100% (1/1), done.
```

Time for action – adding a new node

Before we can run Puppet on the new machine, we need to add a node declaration for it.

1. On the new server, edit `/home/git/puppet/manifests/nodes.pp` and add the following section:

```
node 'demo2' {
  include nginx
}
```

2. Now run Puppet:

```
ubuntu@demo2:~$ sudo puppet apply /home/git/puppet/manifests/site.
pp --modulepath=/home/git/puppet/modules/
Notice: /Stage[main]/Nginx/Package[nginx]/ensure: ensure changed
'purged' to 'present'
Notice: /Stage[main]/Nginx/File[/etc/nginx/sites-enabled/default]/
ensure: defined content as '{md5}0750fd1b8da76b84f2597de76c1b9bce'
Notice: /Stage[main]/Nginx/Service[nginx]/ensure: ensure changed
'stopped' to 'running'
Notice: /Stage[main]/Nginx/Service[nginx]: Triggered 'refresh'
from 1 events
Notice: Finished catalog run in 11.84 seconds
```

Time for action – pushing changes to the master repo

We have made a change to our working copy of the Puppet repo on demo2, but so far we haven't committed and pushed the change to the master repo. We need to do this so that the changes will be available to all other machines using the repo.

1. Commit the changes:

```
ubuntu@demo2:~$ sudo su - git
$ bash
git@demo2:~$ cd puppet
git@demo2:~/puppet$ git status
# On branch master
# Changes not staged for commit:
#   (use "git add <file>..." to update what will be committed)
#   (use "git checkout -- <file>..." to discard changes in working
directory)
#
#   modified:   manifests/nodes.pp
#
no changes added to commit (use "git add" and/or "git commit -a")
git@demo2:~/puppet$ git add manifests/nodes.pp
git@demo2:~/puppet$ git commit -m "Adding node demo2"
--author="john@bitfieldconsulting.com"
[master 967cb8b] Adding node demo2
 ...
 1 file changed, 5 insertions(+)
```

2. Now push all changes back to the master repo:

```
git@demo2:~/puppet$ git push
Counting objects: 7, done.
Compressing objects: 100% (4/4), done.
Writing objects: 100% (4/4), 412 bytes, done.
Total 4 (delta 0), reused 0 (delta 0)
To 23.20.119.201:/var/git/puppet.git
   0ce98c0..967cb8b  master -> master
```

Exercise

If you work as part of a team, have one of your colleagues clone the master repo and make some changes. She'll need the private SSH key you created for `git` (or you can add her SSH public key to the `authorized_keys` file for the `git` user).

Have her push the changes to the master repo, and then update the working copy on the `demo2` box and apply it.

Now everyone in your team can work independently on the Puppet manifests, making and pushing changes, and applying them to all the machines controlled by Puppet.

Pulling changes automatically

You now have your machines set up so that they can receive changes to the Puppet manifests using Git, and those changes can then be applied locally. However, you still have to log into each machine to do this. It would be helpful to have each machine update itself and apply any changes automatically. Then all you need to do is push a change to the repo, and it will go out to all your machines within a certain time.

The simplest way to do this is with a cron job, which updates the repo and then runs Puppet if anything has changed.

Time for action – automatic pull-and-apply script

1. Create the file `/usr/local/bin/pull-updates` with the following contents:

    ```
    #!/bin/sh
    PUPPETDIR=/home/git/puppet
    cd ${PUPPETDIR}
    git pull && sudo /usr/local/bin/papply
    ```

2. Create the file `/usr/local/bin/papply` with the following contents:

    ```
    #!/bin/sh
    PUPPETDIR=/home/git/puppet
    /usr/bin/puppet apply --modulepath ${PUPPETDIR}/modules
    ${PUPPETDIR}/manifests/site.pp
    ```

3. Set execute permissions on both scripts:

    ```
    ubuntu@demo2:~$ sudo chmod a+x /usr/local/bin/pull-updates
    ubuntu@demo2:~$ sudo chmod a+x /usr/local/bin/papply
    ```

4. Edit the `sudoers` file:

    ```
    ubuntu@demo2:~$ sudo visudo
    ```

5. Add the following line to give `git` permission to run the `papply` script as root:

    ```
    git          ALL = (root) NOPASSWD: /usr/local/bin/papply
    ```

6. Test that `git` can run the `papply` script:

    ```
    git@demo2:~$ sudo papply
    Notice: Finished catalog run in 1.88 seconds
    ```

7. Test that `git` can run the `pull-updates` script:

```
git@demo2:~$ pull-updates
Already up-to-date.
Notice: Finished catalog run in 1.80 seconds
```

8. Edit the crontab for `git`:

```
git@demo2:~$ crontab -e
```

9. Add a cron job for `git` to run this script automatically, and save the file:

```
*/10 * * * * /usr/local/bin/pull-updates
```

10. Check that the `git` user's crontab has been updated:

```
git@demo2:~$ crontab -l |grep update
*/10 * * * * /usr/local/bin/pull-updates
```

What just happened?

The `pull-updates` script will now run automatically every 10 minutes. When it runs, it will attempt to execute `git pull` in the Puppet repo directory. If there are no changes to pull, nothing will happen.

If any changes are pulled, the script will go on to run `papply` to apply the changes.

So now whenever you push a change to the master Puppet repo, the `demo2` machine will automatically pick it up and apply it.

Learning more about Git

As you get familiar with Git, or even if you've been using it for a while, you may find it helpful to read the excellent "Pro Git" by Scott Chacon, available online here:

```
http://git-scm.com/book/
```

Summary

A quick rundown of what we've learned in this chapter.

Why version control?

Version control is very useful for tracking changes to any source code, including Puppet manifests. It's especially important when several people are working on the same code, so that they can communicate with one another about their changes. Version control can also detect and alert you to conflicts when the same file is edited by different people independently.

Getting started with Git

To use the Git version control tool, you create a repo using `git init` and make an initial snapshot using `git add` and `git commit`. Thereafter, every time you want to record a set of changes, use `git add` and `git commit` again to store them with an appropriate message.

As you're working on a set of changes, you can see how the current code differs from Git's stored version using `git diff`. The `git status` command will show you which files Git thinks may need to be committed.

You can see the complete history of changes to your repo using the `git log` command. `git whatchanged` will show you the differences in each file before and after the commit.

Networking Puppet

The problem of distributing your Puppet manifests securely and efficiently to a number of machines can be solved in several ways. The traditional way is to use a special extra server called a **Puppetmaster**, which authenticates all the other machines and gives them their manifests. For small infrastructures, this is overkill; for large infrastructures, it's slow. Consequently, I usually recommend a different approach: using Git as the distribution mechanism.

Using Git to distribute your Puppet manifests to multiple machines is a simple, reliable, and scalable alternative to using a Puppetmaster. All you need is a Git repo from which each machine clones its own working copy and runs Puppet locally via a cron job.

An easy way to make this secure is to use Git over SSH, with a private key you distribute to each machine that is authorized to pull Puppet manifests.

Since it's a very good idea to use Git anyway, to manage changes to your Puppet code, and to enable your team members to work on the Puppet manifests in a distributed way, this is simply a logical extension of that idea.

You don't need an extra server (which would in any case be a single point of failure), and it also makes it easy for you to test changes and upgrades using Git branches.

You can set up a script to pull updates from Git and run Puppet automatically if there are any changes. It's a good idea to trigger the script to run at intervals using `cron`.

5

Managing users

The real problem isn't whether machines think but whether people do.

— *B.F. Skinner*

In this chapter, you'll learn how to use Puppet to create and manage user accounts, configure SSH access and keys, and control user privileges via sudo.

Users

One of the most common system administration tasks is setting up user accounts. We'll see how Puppet can help with this in a moment, but first a word about the kind of user configuration we should be aiming for.

Security and access control

Organizations with good security and access control practices tend to use some or all of the following policies:

♦ Everyone who needs access to a machine has her own user account with an SSH key (not a password)

♦ Access to special-purpose accounts, such as those used to deploy and run applications, or a database, is controlled by authorizing specific SSH keys, rather than using passwords

♦ Accounts that need certain, specific superuser privileges can get them via the sudo mechanism

♦ The root account is not accessible via the network (but there is secure, out-of-band access to the system console)

♦ Third parties, such as contractors and support staff, get temporary access with limited privileges, which can be revoked once a job is finished

Setting up policies like these, while highly desirable from a security point of view, is time-consuming to do by hand and difficult to maintain. If a new user arrives, someone has to add and configure his account on every server. If a user leaves, the accounts have to be removed or locked everywhere.

It's not surprising that many organizations, under time pressure and needing things to work right away, don't bother too much about security and access control. In many cases the simplest thing to do is for everyone to log in as root using the same password, often for all machines. Even if there are official policies about security, people often don't follow them, because it's more convenient to do things an insecure way.

What Puppet can do

One of the biggest wins that Puppet can deliver in an organization is making it quick and easy to manage user accounts securely across a large network. You can add or remove individual and shared accounts, control their access via SSH, manage their privileges via sudo, and have the changes immediately applied to every machine under Puppet's control, all without logging into a single server.

When this is the case, it's much easier to ensure that security policies are followed, without hindering people from doing their jobs. When your SSH key works everywhere, you don't need to share or write down passwords, and when your account has the necessary privileges, you don't need to use root. So everybody benefits.

Puppet provides a number of ways to help you manage users. The user resource type controls user accounts, and the ssh_authorized_key resource type controls SSH access to accounts. You can use Puppet to control user privileges by managing the sudoers file, and you can also replace the default SSH configuration file with a more secure version managed by Puppet.

In the rest of this chapter, we'll see how to use these techniques, again using our cat-pictures.com example site.

Time for action – creating a user

There's a new developer on the cat-pictures project, named Art Vandelay. You'll need to create a user account for him on the server using Puppet.

1. Edit your manifests/nodes.pp file as follows:

```
node 'demo' {
  user { 'art':
    ensure     => present,
    comment    => 'Art Vandelay',
    home       => '/home/art',
    managehome => true,
  }
}
```

2. Apply the manifest:

```
ubuntu@demo:~/puppet$ papply
Notice:/Stage[main]//Node[demo]/User[art]/ensure: created
Notice: Finished catalog run in 0.25 seconds
```

3. Make sure the user has been created correctly:

```
ubuntu@demo:~/puppet$ sudo su - art
$ pwd
/home/art
```

What just happened?

Puppet's `user` resource type creates a user (or modifies it if the user already exists). The following line declares a user whose login name is `art`:

```
user { 'art':
```

The user should be present:

```
ensure      => present,
```

We can also specify here some information about the user:

```
comment => 'Art Vandelay',
```

The `comment` attribute sets the user's full name.

```
home      => '/home/art',
```

The `home` attribute sets the path to the user's home directory. Puppet will not create this directory for you unless you also set the `managehome` attribute:

```
managehome => true,
```

So the manifest says that a user named `art` should exist, whose full name is Art Vandelay, and that his home directory should be `/home/art`, and that that directory should exist.

> Note that we have not specified a password for the user, and as a result `art` will not yet be able to log in. Although Puppet can set passwords for users (with the `password` attribute) I recommend you use **SSH authentication** instead, which is much more secure than using a password. We'll see how to do this later in the *Access control* section.

Removing user accounts

To remove a user from the system altogether, use the `ensure => absent` attribute:

```
user { 'art':
  ensure => absent,
}
```

When you run Puppet, the `art` account will be removed (though Art's home directory and any files he owned will remain).

Just removing the `user` resource declaration from your Puppet code won't actually remove the user's account from your machines. If you think about it, this makes sense. Otherwise, Puppet would remove all accounts it hasn't been specifically told about, including `root`!

So when you want to remove a user, change their `ensure` attribute from `present` to `absent`, and Puppet will delete the account for you. Once this change has been applied to all machines, you can remove the `user` declaration from your Puppet manifest.

Access control

Having created the user's account, we now need to provide a secure way for him to log in. We can do this using the SSH protocol.

What is SSH?

SSH is a more secure way of controlling user access than the traditional "username and password" approach. Instead of using a password, which the user has to keep secret, it uses two pieces of information: the **public** key and the **private** key. Only the private key has to be secret. You can put your public key on any computer, or publish it to the world if you like. But no one can log in to an account controlled by your public key unless they also have the matching private key.

This has the pleasant consequence that you only need one SSH key, and you can use it for everything. It's a very bad idea to use the same password for multiple accounts, but with SSH, that's no problem. So long as you keep the private key secret, you can use your public key everywhere.

Managing SSH keys

Puppet can manage SSH public keys and authorize them for user accounts, using the `ssh_authorized_key` resource type.

Time for action – adding an SSH authorized key

1. You'll need your own SSH public key for this. If you already have one on your own computer, display the contents:

```
john@T-Bone:~$ cat ~/.ssh/id_rsa.pub

ssh-rsa AAAAB3NzaC1yc2EAAAABIwAAAIEA3ATqENg+GWACa2B
zeqTdGnJhNoBer8x6pfWkzNzeM8Zx7/2Tf2pl7kHdbsiTXEUawq
zXZQtZzt/j3Oya+PZjcRpWNRzprSmd2UxEEPTqDw9LqY5S2B8og/
NyzWaIYPsKoatcgC7VgYHplcTbzEhGu8BsoEVBGYu3IRy5RkAcZik=
```

2. If you don't have an SSH key, you can generate one for this exercise:

```
ubuntu@demo:~$ ssh-keygen

Generating public/private rsa key pair.

Enter file in which to save the key (/home/ubuntu/.ssh/id_rsa):

Enter passphrase (empty for no passphrase):

Enter same passphrase again:

Your identification has been saved in /home/ubuntu/.ssh/id_rsa.

Your public key has been saved in /home/ubuntu/.ssh/id_rsa.pub.
```

3. Now display the `id_rsa.pub` file to see the public key:

```
ubuntu@demo:~$ cat /home/ubuntu/.ssh/id_rsa.pub

ssh-rsa

CveowByzhgEFMOXi7Ycxr1h958BjVyqGRUTkSoz8bfjqeXmJAvM1/5V3sT1/YV9r9y
sM7Rzu7K51YB+Bg6CQr0QJjABev56rTsbVtyAHi7Ju9zfu6JJ7pfnSfKajwBpHSW0e
yTYm8Fnkry920ikoeQOwN+DsYt5NY3h+sPISb98oXRWe0EetFanJ8AwlUuYQ9DmO+3
kArMyyT

IzgWR7wE6SMKG5RujzWk0Hb7ngGWyjXJtG7F3k3SD06W3UmGPK1AXPRbW4vJDL+hhL
ubuntu@

6FtxIzgWR7wE6SMKG5RujzWk0Hb7ngGWyjXJtG7F3k3SD06W3UmGPK1AXPRbW4vJDL
+hhL ubuntu@demo
```

The key itself is the long string of numbers and letters, without the `ssh-rsa` part at the beginning, or the `ubuntu@demo` part at the end. It's this string you'll put into the Puppet manifest in the next step.

4. Edit your `manifests/nodes.pp` file as follows (using your own key string as the value for key):

```
node 'demo' {
  user { 'art':
    ensure      => present,
    comment     => 'Art Vandelay',
    home        => '/home/art',
    managehome  => true,
```

```
    }
  ssh_authorized_key { 'art_ssh':
    user => 'art',
    type => 'rsa',
    key  => 'AAAAB3NzaC1yc2EAAAABIwAAAIEA3ATqENg+GWAC
  a2BzeqTdGnJhNoBer8x6pfWkzNzeM8Zx7/2Tf2pl7kHdbsiTXEUaw
  qzXZQtZzt/j3Oya+PZjcRpWNRzprSmd2UxEEPTqDw9LqY5S2B8og/
  NyzWaIYPsKoatcgC7VgYHplcTbzEhGu8BsoEVBGYu3IRy5RkAcZik=',
    }
  }
```

5. Run Puppet:

```
ubuntu@demo:~/puppet$ papply
Notice: /Stage[main]//Node[demo]/Ssh_authorized_key[art_ssh]/
ensure: created
Notice: Finished catalog run in 0.05 seconds
```

6. Now test that you have access to the `art` account using this key. On a machine that has your SSH key, run the following command:

```
$ ssh art@demo
Welcome to Ubuntu 12.04.1 LTS (GNU/Linux 3.2.0-29-virtual x86_64)
```

What just happened?

The following line declares an `ssh_authorized_key` resource:

```
  ssh_authorized_key { 'art_ssh':
```

The name (`art_ssh` in this case) can be anything you like, so long as it's unique. It will be added as a comment at the end of the key in the `authorized_keys` file.

We need to specify the user account for which this key will grant access:

```
  user => 'art',
```

We also have to tell Puppet the key type (`rsa` or `dsa`; you'll know which it is because the key file itself contains `ssh-rsa` or `ssh-dsa` at the beginning):

```
  type => 'rsa',
```

And lastly the key string, which in this case should be your own key instead of mine:

```
  key  => 'AAAAB3NzaC1yc2EAAAABIwAAAIEA3ATqENg+GWACa2B
  zeqTdGnJhNoBer8x6pfWkzNzeM8Zx7/2Tf2pl7kHdbsiTXEUawq
  zXZQtZzt/j3Oya+PZjcRpWNRzprSmd2UxEEPTqDw9LqY5S2B8og/
  NyzWaIYPsKoatcgC7VgYHplcTbzEhGu8BsoEVBGYu3IRy5RkAcZik=',
```

Puppet will then add this key to the file /home/art/.ssh/authorized_keys. When you try to log in to Art's account via SSH, the system will look in this file to see if your private key matches any of the public keys listed there. Assuming it does, you'll be able to log in.

Generating new SSH keys

For managing users other than yourself, you can generate new keys for them using the ssh-keygen command:

```
ubuntu@demo:~/puppet$ ssh-keygen -f fabian
Generating public/private rsa key pair.
Enter passphrase (empty for no passphrase):
Enter same passphrase again:
Your identification has been saved in fabian.
Your public key has been saved in fabian.pub.
```

Give the user the secret key file (fabian) and put the matching public key into Puppet as an ssh_authorized_key resource for that user.

Special-purpose keys

Sometimes an automatic process on one machine needs access to another machine. For example, you might have a daily cron job that uploads logs to a central storage server. So how do you manage this securely?

One simple way is to create a user account on the target machine dedicated to the purpose: log uploading, for example. This account is secured with SSH, and access is restricted to a special private key that you create. The private key is distributed with Puppet to only those machines that need it, and can be removed or changed at any time.

This is exactly the approach we took in an earlier chapter for setting up automatic access to a Git server, so that machines can pull their Puppet config at regular intervals and apply changes. You can use this idea to manage access for any automated task.

For even greater security, you can give each machine its own private key, and authorize the target machine for all the corresponding public keys.

Locking user accounts

If you want to be able to block a user from logging in, you can do this by temporarily removing his SSH key in Puppet:

```
ssh_authorized_key { 'art_ssh':
  user => 'art',
```

```
    type => 'rsa',
    key  => '',
}
```

The value for `key` in the example above is an empty single-quoted string (`''`). This will disable SSH logins for the user. If you have enabled password authentication (which I don't recommend, but you might need it in some situations) then this won't stop the user from logging in using his password. To do this, set a password of a single star (`*`) in Puppet:

```
user { 'art':
    ensure     => present,
    comment    => 'Art Vandelay',
    home       => '/home/art',
    managehome => true,
    password   => '*',
}
```

This will block the user from logging in via password (though SSH will still work unless you also disable that, as shown above). To unlock the account, remove the `password` attribute and re-set the user's password using the `passwd` command.

Managing SSH configuration

Although it's not necessary if you just want to set up user accounts with SSH keys, you can use Puppet to manage the global SSH configuration for your system, for example, to allow only a specified list of users to log in. We'll see how to do that in the following section.

Time for action – deploying an SSH configuration file

1. Create the directories needed for a new `ssh` module:

```
ubuntu@demo:~/puppet$ mkdir modules/ssh
ubuntu@demo:~/puppet$ mkdir modules/ssh/manifests
ubuntu@demo:~/puppet$ mkdir modules/ssh/files
```

2. Create the file `modules/ssh/manifests/init.pp` with the following contents:

```
# Manage the SSH service
class ssh {
  service { 'ssh':
    ensure => running,
  }

  file { '/etc/ssh/sshd_config':
    source => 'puppet:///modules/ssh/sshd_config',
    notify => Service['ssh'],
```

```
        owner  => 'root',
        group  => 'root',
    }
}
```

3. Create the file `modules/ssh/files/sshd_config` with the following contents (if you're not logging in as `ubuntu`, add the user you're logging in as to the list of `AllowUsers`. Only the named users will be able to log in once you've applied this change with Puppet, so be careful):

```
Port 22
Protocol 2
PermitRootLogin no
PasswordAuthentication no
AllowUsers ubuntu art
UsePAM yes
```

4. Add this to your node definition in `manifests/nodes.pp`:

```
include ssh
```

5. Run Puppet:

```
ubuntu@demo:~/puppet$ papply
```

Notice: /Stage[main]/Ssh/File[/etc/ssh/sshd_config]/content: content changed '{md5}5f15065f987c4d9851ad3448d4aadfa6' to '{md5}6 e96247a35996ba5adc36acbf34faf9b'

Notice: /Stage[main]/Ssh/Service[ssh]: Triggered 'refresh' from 1 events

Notice: Finished catalog run in 0.23 seconds

6. Check that you can still log in from another machine as `ubuntu` or `art`:

```
john@T-Bone:~$ ssh ubuntu@demo
```

Welcome to Ubuntu 12.04.1 LTS (GNU/Linux 3.2.0-29-virtual x86_64)

User privileges

Linux and other UNIX-like operating systems commonly have two levels of user privilege: the `root` user, who can edit system files and perform operations tasks, such as rebooting the machine, and normal users, who can only edit and read files owned by themselves, and have no special privileges. This ensures that users don't get access to files or commands that they shouldn't have. However, sometimes you need to grant special privileges to a user, without giving her full access to the `root` account. You can do this using a UNIX command called `sudo`.

sudo

The sudo command allows normal users to run commands with root privileges, if this is specifically authorized by the system administrator. For example, a developer user might be given privileges to run service nginx restart as root.

The set of users allowed to assume root privileges, and the specific commands they can run, is specified in the file /etc/sudoers. We can use Puppet to manage this file, and thus control user privileges on the machine.

Time for action – deploying a sudoers file

1. Create the directories for a sudoers module:

   ```
   ubuntu@demo:~/puppet$ mkdir modules/sudoers
   ubuntu@demo:~/puppet$ mkdir modules/sudoers/manifests
   ubuntu@demo:~/puppet$ mkdir modules/sudoers/files
   ```

2. Create the file modules/sudoers/manifests/init.pp with the following contents:

   ```
   # Manage the sudoers file
   class sudoers {
     file { '/etc/sudoers':
       source => 'puppet:///modules/sudoers/sudoers',
       mode   => '0440',
       owner  => 'root',
       group  => 'root',
     }
   }
   ```

3. Create the file modules/sudoers/files/sudoers with the following contents:

   ```
   # User privilege specification
   root    ALL = (ALL) ALL
   ubuntu  ALL = (ALL) NOPASSWD:ALL
   art     ALL = (ALL) NOPASSWD: /bin/ls
   ```

4. Check the syntax of the sudoers file:

   ```
   ubuntu@demo:~/puppet$ visudo -c -f modules/sudoers/files/sudoers
   modules/sudoers/files/sudoers: parsed OK
   ```

5. If there are any errors, correct them before moving on. If you use Puppet to deploy a `sudoers` file that contains syntax errors, no users will be able to `sudo` anything, and you will need to log in as `root` in order to fix the problem. So whenever you make a change to Puppet's copy of the `sudoers` file, use the `visudo` command as above to check the syntax.

6. Add this to your node definition in `manifests/nodes.pp`:

```
include sudoers
```

7. Run Puppet:

```
ubuntu@demo:~/puppet$ papply

Notice: /Stage[main]/Sudoers/File[/etc/sudoers]/content: content
changed '{md5}5755c84fcb480985818c6daa9faa386c' to '{md5}
f9d8dbf9b36280c3e860af7eede92fd1'

Notice: Finished catalog run in 0.10 seconds
```

8. Run the following command as the `ubuntu` user to verify that the changes have taken effect:

```
ubuntu@demo:~/puppet$ sudo whoami

root
```

9. Run the following command as the `art` user, to test whether he has the privilege to run `/bin/ls` as `root`:

```
art@demo:~$ sudo /bin/ls -l /

total 80

drwxr-xr-x  2 root root  4096 Aug 22 05:49 bin

drwxr-xr-x  3 root root  4096 Jan  9 13:54 boot

drwxr-xr-x 12 root root  3840 Jan  9 13:47 dev

drwxr-xr-x 89 root root  4096 Jan 14 15:29 etc

drwxr-xr-x  3 root root  4096 Aug 22 05:48 home
```

What just happened?

When you use Puppet to deploy the `sudoers` file, the privilege settings listed in the file will immediately take effect. When any user runs a command using `sudo`, the system will consult `/etc/sudoers` to see whether or not the command is allowed.

The line `root     ALL = (ALL) ALL` allows user `root` to sudo any command as root (this might seem unnecessary, but it's included for consistency, and to make sure any scripts that use `sudo` don't suddenly fail if run as `root`).

The line ubuntu ALL = (ALL) NOPASSWD:ALL allows user ubuntu to run any command, on any system, as any user, without having to enter a password. (You can have sudo require the user's password, if you use passwords, to make things a little more secure. Generally though, sudoers entries are used for scripts and automated jobs that can't enter a password anyway.)

The line art ALL = (ALL) NOPASSWD: /bin/ls is more specific. It allows user art to run only the command /bin/ls (with any arguments). No other commands will work:

```
art@demo:~$ sudo /sbin/halt
[sudo] password for art:
Sorry, user art is not allowed to execute '/sbin/halt' as root on
demo.
```

Summary

A quick rundown of what we've learned in this chapter.

Security practices

If you follow good security practices for your network, each user should have her own named account with SSH (not password) access. Any special-purpose accounts should be authorized for the SSH keys of the specific users that need access to them. Login as root should be disallowed (except on a secure console).

User resources

Puppet can manage users directly using the user resource:

```
user { 'art':
  ensure => present,
  ...
}
```

You can specify the user's full name with the comment attribute:

```
comment    => 'Art Vandelay',
```

Create a home directory with the home and managehome attributes:

```
home        => '/home/art',
managehome => true,
```

Removing or locking accounts

To remove a user, change `ensure` to absent:

```
user { 'art':
  ensure => absent,
  ...
}
```

Just removing the user resource from Puppet won't remove the user account from the server, so if you need to delete the account, make sure you use `ensure => absent`.

To lock an account, for example to temporarily disable access, set the `ssh_authorized_key` to an empty string and the `password` to a * character.

Managing SSH keys

You can control the SSH keys authorized to log into the user's account using the `ssh_authorized_key` resource type:

```
ssh_authorized_key { 'art_ssh':
  ...
}
```

Specify the key metadata with the `user`, `type`, and `key` attributes:

```
user => 'art',
type => 'rsa',
key  => 'AAAAB3...',
```

If you need to generate new SSH keys for users, you can do it with the `ssh-keygen` command:

```
ssh-keygen -f fabian
```

Configuring SSH

Puppet can also manage global SSH configuration by deploying the `/etc/ssh/sshd_config` file. You can limit the list of users allowed to log in by specifying the `AllowUsers` parameter in this file:

```
AllowUsers ubuntu art
```

Managing privileges with sudo

User privileges, and permission for normal users to run certain commands as root, are controlled by the /etc/sudoers file. By managing this file (carefully) with Puppet you can control all user sudo rights on a machine, using a syntax like this:

```
# User privilege specification
root   ALL = (ALL) ALL
ubuntu  ALL = (ALL) NOPASSWD:ALL
art     ALL = (ALL) NOPASSWD: /bin/ls
```

6
Tasks and templates

You can tell whether a man is clever by his answers. You can tell whether a man is wise by his questions.

— Naguib Mahfouz

In this chapter, you'll learn how to use Puppet's resource types to run commands, schedule regular tasks, and distribute large trees of files. You'll also find out how to insert values dynamically into files using templates.

Running commands with exec resources

We've seen that Puppet lets you model various aspects of a system using resources, such as user or file resources. You describe how the system should be configured, and Puppet will run appropriate commands behind the scenes to bring about the desired state.

But what if you want Puppet to run a certain command directly? You can do this using an exec resource. This is a very flexible and powerful resource, and you can use it to implement almost anything in Puppet. In this section we'll see how to get the most from exec resources.

Time for action – running an arbitrary command

1. Modify your manifests/nodes.pp file as follows:

    ```
    node 'demo' {
      exec { 'Run my arbitrary command':
        command => '/bin/echo I ran this command on `/bin/date` >/tmp/
    command.output.txt',
      }
    }
    ```

2. Run Puppet:

    ```
    ubuntu@demo:~/puppet$ papply

    Notice: /Stage[main]//Node[demo]/Exec[Run my arbitrary command]/
    returns: executed successfully

    Notice: Finished catalog run in 0.14 seconds
    ```

3. Check the output produced (you won't see exactly the same date and time shown here, unless you're a Time Lord):

    ```
    ubuntu@demo:~/puppet$ cat /tmp/command.output.txt

    I ran this command on Mon Dec 17 16:14:04 UTC 2012
    ```

What just happened?

The line exec { 'Run my arbitrary command': declares an exec resource with the name Run my arbitrary command. The name can be anything; it's not otherwise used by Puppet, except that like all resource names it can't be the same as another instance of the same resource type.

The command to run is specified by the following line:

```
command => '/bin/echo I ran this command on `/bin/date` >/tmp/command.
output.txt',
```

Note that the UNIX commands, `echo` and `date`, are specified with their full path. This is because Puppet wants to be sure exactly which command you mean.

When Puppet runs, it applies the `exec` resource by running the command:

```
/bin/echo I ran this command on `/bin/date` >/tmp/command.output.txt
```

This command will write the following text to `/tmp/command.output.txt`:

```
I ran this command on Mon Dec 17 16:14:04 UTC 2012
```

Running commands selectively

The `exec` resource we've created will be applied every time Puppet runs, but that's not always what we want. Say we are using an `exec` resource to download a file, for example. Once the file is downloaded the first time we don't need to do it again. Here's an example:

```
exec { 'Download public key for John':
  cwd     => '/tmp',
  command => '/usr/bin/wget http://bitfieldconsulting.com/files/john.
pub',
  creates => '/tmp/john.pub',
}
```

The `creates` attribute specifies the full path to a file. Puppet will check to see if this file already exists. If it does, the `exec` won't be run. This is a neat way to have a command run only if it is needed, and not otherwise.

 Did you notice we also added the `cwd` attribute? This tells Puppet the directory in which to run the command (**cwd** stands for **current working directory**), so that any files created by the command, like `john.pub` in this example, will end up in that directory.

You can also use the `unless` or `onlyif` attributes to control when an `exec` is run. `unless` or `onlyif` both specify a command for Puppet to run to test whether the `exec` needs to be applied.

The exit status of the test command determines what Puppet should do. For example:

```
exec { 'add-cloudera-apt-key':
  command => '/usr/bin/apt-key add /tmp/cloudera.pub',
  unless  => '/usr/bin/apt-key list |grep Cloudera',
}
```

Here, we're using an `exec` to add an APT repository key to the system keyring. This only needs to be done once, so the `unless` command checks whether the key has already been added. If the `grep` succeeds, we know the key is already present, so we don't need to do anything. The exit status will be zero, so Puppet won't apply the `exec`. On the other hand, if the `grep` fails, the exit status will be non-zero so Puppet will apply the `exec`.

Using `onlyif`, the opposite logic applies; the `exec` will be run only if the test command succeeds (exits with a zero status).

Triggering commands

Another way to control when an `exec` is run is to use the `refreshonly` attribute:

```
exec { 'icinga-config-check':
  command     => '/usr/sbin/icinga -v /etc/icinga/icinga.cfg && /usr/
sbin/service icinga restart',
  refreshonly => true,
  subscribe   => File['/etc/icinga/icinga.cfg'],
}
```

When `refreshonly` is set, Puppet will not apply the `exec` unless it's triggered by `subscribe` or `notify` from some other resource. In this example, the `exec` subscribes to the file `/etc/icinga/icinga.cfg`. If this file changes, Puppet will run the `exec`, but not otherwise.

This is a very useful pattern when you want to take some action if a config file changes, especially if you want to sanity-check the file's contents (as in the example) before restarting the service that reads it.

Chaining commands

Often you have a series of commands that need to run in a particular order (for example, if you're installing software from source, you might need to download a file, unpack it, build it, and install it). To do this, for short sequences, you can use the shell `&&` construct as shown in the preceding example:

```
/usr/sbin/icinga -v /etc/icinga/icinga.cfg && /usr/sbin/service icinga
restart
```

This will chain the commands together in the order you specify, bailing out if any of the commands fail.

For more complicated sequences, or where you may also need to trigger individual commands from other resources, you can use the `require` attribute to specify the ordering explicitly:

```
exec { 'command-1':
  command => '/bin/echo Step 1',
}

exec { 'command-2':
  command => '/bin/echo Step 2',
  require => Exec['command-1'],
}

exec { 'command-3':
  command => '/bin/echo Step 3',
  require => Exec['command-2'],
}
```

Command search paths

As we've seen, Puppet requires us to specify the full path to any command referenced in an `exec` resource. However, if you like, you can provide a list of paths for Puppet to search for commands, using the `path` attribute. For example:

```
exec { 'Run my arbitrary command':
  command => 'echo I ran this command on `date` >/tmp/command.output.
txt',
  path    => ['/bin', '/usr/bin'],
}
```

Now when Puppet sees a command name, it will search the directories you specify looking for the matching commands.

If you want to specify a set of default search paths for all `exec` resources, you can put this in your `site.pp` file:

```
Exec {
  path => ['/bin', '/usr/bin'],
}
```

Note the capital E for Exec. This means "make this the default for all exec resources." Then you can use unqualified commands without an explicit path attribute:

```
exec { 'Run my arbitrary command':
  command => 'echo I ran this command on `date` >/tmp/command.output.
txt',
}
```

Puppet will use the default paths you specified: /bin and /usr/bin.

Scheduled tasks

Typically, when you want a command to be run at a certain time of day, or at regular intervals, you can use the UNIX cron facility. For example, a backup job might run every night at 4 a.m., or a queue processing task might run every 5 minutes.

Puppet can manage cron jobs directly using the cron resource type. Here's an example.

Time for action – scheduling a backup

1. Modify your manifests/nodes.pp file as follows:

```
node 'demo' {
  cron { 'Back up cat-pictures':
    command => '/usr/bin/rsync -az /var/www/cat-pictures/ /cat-
pictures-backup/',
    hour    => '04',
    minute  => '00',
  }
}
```

2. Run Puppet:

```
ubuntu@demo:~/puppet$ papply
Notice: /Stage[main]//Node[demo]/Cron[Back up cat-pictures]/
ensure: created
Notice: Finished catalog run in 0.12 seconds
```

3. Check that the cron job was correctly configured:

```
ubuntu@demo:~/puppet$ sudo crontab -l
# HEADER: This file was autogenerated on Tue Dec 18 12:50:11 +0000
2012 by puppet.
```

```
# HEADER: While it can still be managed manually, it is definitely
not recommended.

# HEADER: Note particularly that the comments starting with
'Puppet Name' should

# HEADER: not be deleted, as doing so could cause duplicate cron
jobs.

# Puppet Name: Back up cat-pictures

0 4 * * * /usr/bin/rsync -avz /var/www/cat-pictures/ /cat-
pictures-backup/
```

What just happened?

The line cron { 'Back up cat-pictures': declares a cron resource named Back up
cat-pictures (as with exec resources, the name doesn't matter, but it must be unique).

```
command => '/usr/bin/rsync -avz /var/www/cat-pictures/ /cat-pictures-
backup/',
```

The preceding line sets the command to run (in this case, an rsync command to back up
all files and directories under /var/www/cat-pictures to /cat-pictures-backup).
As with exec resources, commands need to be qualified with their full path.

We now go on to specify the time at which the job should run.

```
hour     => '04',
```

This is in 24-hour format, with 00 being midnight, and 23 being 11 p.m.

```
minute   => '00',
```

If minute is not specified, it defaults to *; that is, it runs every minute! So always
specify both hour and minute (if there is no hour, the job runs every hour at the
minute you specify).

> Note that Puppet adds a helpful header to the crontab file, warning you
> not to meddle in the affairs of Puppet. In fact, you can safely add, remove,
> and modify any cron jobs not managed by Puppet. Puppet identifies the
> cron jobs it's managing by the Puppet Name comment above each job.
> So, as the warning suggests, don't remove or edit these comments or
> Puppet will think the job is missing and add a new copy of it.

More scheduling options

The `cron` resources can have several other attributes to set the time for the scheduled job:

- `weekday` – the day of the week, for example, Friday
- `month` – not often used, but can be used to run jobs only during a specific month, for example, January
- `monthday` – the day of the month, for example 1 to run a job on the first day of each month

If any of these attributes are not supplied, they default to `*`; that is, every weekday, every month, or every day of the month.

Running jobs at regular intervals

If you want to run a job every 5 minutes, say, you can specify an interval such as this:

```
minute => '*/5',
hour    => '*',
```

You can use the same pattern with the other time attributes, for example, to run a job every 6 hours on the hour:

```
hour    => '*/6',
minute => '00',
```

Running a job as a specified user

The default user for cron jobs is `root`, but if you want to run the job as a different user, just give the `cron` resource a `user` attribute:

```
user => 'www-data',
```

The job will be added to the crontab file for `www-data`.

Exercise

Use a `cron` resource to automate the `pull-updates` job you set up in *Chapter 4, Managing Puppet with Git*, which automatically pulls Git changes and applies Puppet on each machine. Make this part of every machine's base configuration.

Distributing files

We've seen in previous chapters how to use Puppet's `file` resource to deploy a single file to a server. Sometimes, though, you need to copy a whole directory tree of files, without having to list each individual file in your Puppet manifest. The `recurse` attribute allows you to do this. We'll see how to use it in the next example.

Time for action – using a recursive file resource

The `cat-pictures` application is nearly complete, but it needs some pictures of cats added in time for the launch. The art department has sent over a set of feline stock photos for you to deploy to the website.

1. Create the directories for a new cat-pictures module:

```
ubuntu@demo:~/puppet$ mkdir modules/cat-pictures
ubuntu@demo:~/puppet$ mkdir modules/cat-pictures/files
```

2. Create a directory for the images, and some placeholder image files (for extra credit, download some real pictures of cats from the Internet):

```
ubuntu@demo:~/puppet$ mkdir modules/cat-pictures/files/img
ubuntu@demo:~/puppet$ mkdir modules/cat-pictures/files/img/
cat_001.jpg
ubuntu@demo:~/puppet$ mkdir modules/cat-pictures/files/img/
cat_002.jpg
ubuntu@demo:~/puppet$ mkdir modules/cat-pictures/files/img/
cat_003.jpg
```

3. Modify your `manifests/nodes.pp` file as follows:

```
node 'demo' {
  file { '/var/www/cat-pictures':
    ensure => directory,
  }

  file { '/var/www/cat-pictures/img':
    source  => 'puppet:///modules/cat-pictures/img',
    recurse => true,
    require => File['/var/www/cat-pictures'],
  }
}
```

4. Run Puppet:

```
ubuntu@demo:~/puppet$ papply
Notice: /Stage[main]//Node[demo]/File[/var/www/cat-pictures]/
ensure: created
Notice: /Stage[main]//Node[demo]/File[/var/www/cat-pictures/img]/
ensure: created
Notice: /File[/var/www/cat-pictures/img/cat_002.jpg]/ensure:
created
Notice: /File[/var/www/cat-pictures/img/cat_001.jpg]/ensure:
created
Notice: /File[/var/www/cat-pictures/img/cat_003.jpg]/ensure:
created
Notice: Finished catalog run in 0.08 seconds
```

What just happened?

First we created a top-level directory for the site files to live in:

```
file { '/var/www/cat-pictures':
  ensure => directory,
}
```

We haven't seen a `file` resource before without either a `source` or a `content` attribute. `ensure => directory` will create a directory, as you might expect. If you said `ensure => present` instead, with no other attributes, Puppet would create an empty file.

The following code is the part that does the heavy lifting:

```
file { '/var/www/cat-pictures/img':
  source  => 'puppet:///modules/cat-pictures/img',
  recurse => true,
  require => File['/var/www/cat-pictures'],
}
```

The `source` attribute is as you've used it before, but the `recurse => true` attribute tells Puppet to copy all files and directories contained in the source. This includes our handful of cat pictures, but it could be thousands of files in a tree of directories many levels deep.

In practice Puppet is rather slow to manage large file trees, because it has to examine every file in the tree on every run to determine if it is up to date with the source. In this situation, you might be better off using Git, for example, to manage large trees of files.

Using templates

In a previous example we had Puppet deploy an Nginx virtual host file for the cat-pictures application. In this case we simply used a file resource with the cat-pictures.conf file distributed from Puppet.

If we wanted to generalize this solution to manage many different websites, it would quickly become tedious to supply an almost identical virtual host file for each site, altering only the name and domain of the site.

What we would prefer is to give Puppet a **template** file into which it could just insert these variables for each different site. The template function serves just this purpose. Anywhere you have multiple files that differ only slightly, or files that need to contain dynamic information, you can use a template.

Time for action – templating an Nginx virtual host

Things are looking up at cat-pictures.com headquarters. They've just got VC funding to build three new sites: dog-pictures.com, hamster-pictures.com, and fish-pictures.com. To prepare for this, your job is to change the Puppet config for cat-pictures.com to use a template, so that you can later use the same template for the new sites.

1. Modify the modules/nginx/manifests/init.pp file as follows:

```
# Manage nginx webserver
class nginx {
  package { 'nginx':
    ensure => installed,
  }

  service { 'nginx':
    ensure  => running,
    enable  => true,
    require => Package['nginx'],
  }

  file { '/etc/nginx/sites-enabled/default':
    ensure => absent,
  }
}
```

2. Create a new `templates` directory in the `nginx` module:

```
ubuntu@demo:~/puppet$ mkdir modules/nginx/templates
```

3. Create the file `modules/nginx/templates/vhost.conf.erb` with the following contents:

```
server {
    listen 80;
    root /var/www/<%= @site_name %>;
    server_name <%= @site_domain %>;
}
```

4. Modify your `manifests/nodes.pp` file as follows:

```
node 'demo' {
    include nginx

    $site_name = 'cat-pictures'
    $site_domain = 'cat-pictures.com'
    file { '/etc/nginx/sites-enabled/cat-pictures.conf':
        content => template('nginx/vhost.conf.erb'),
        notify  => Service['nginx'],
    }
}
```

5. Run Puppet:

```
ubuntu@demo:~/puppet$ papply
Notice:/Stage[main]//Node[demo]/File[/etc/nginx/sites-enabled/cat-
pictures.conf]/ensure: defined content as '{md5}0750fd1b8da76b84f2
597de76c1b9bce'
Notice: /Stage[main]/Nginx/File[/etc/nginx/sites-enabled/default]/
ensure: removed
Notice: /Stage[main]/Nginx/Service[nginx]: Triggered 'refresh'
from 1 events
Notice: Finished catalog run in 0.74 seconds
```

6. Check the resulting virtual host file:

```
ubuntu@demo:~/puppet$ cat /etc/nginx/sites-enabled/cat-pictures.
conf
server {
    listen 80;
    root /var/www/cat-pictures;
    server_name cat-pictures.com;
}
```

What just happened?

First some housekeeping; we previously used the file `/etc/nginx/sites-enabled/default` as the virtual host for `cat-pictures.com`, so we need to remove that:

```
file { '/etc/nginx/sites-enabled/default':
  ensure => absent,
}
```

We create a template file for the virtual host definition:

```
server {
  listen 80;
  root /var/www/<%= @site_name %>;
  server_name <%= @site_domain %>;
}
```

The `<%= %>` signs mark where parameters will go; we will supply `site_name` and `site_domain` later, when we use the template. Puppet will replace `<%= @site_name %>` with the value of the `site_name` variable.

Then in the `nodes.pp` file, we include the `nginx` module on the node:

```
node 'demo' {
  include nginx
```

Before using the template, we need to set values for the variables `site_name` and `site_domain`:

```
$site_name = 'cat-pictures'

$site_domain = 'cat-pictures.com'
```

Note that when we refer to these variables in Puppet code, we use a `$` prefix (`$site_name`), but in the template it's an `@` prefix (`@site_name`). This is because in templates we're actually writing Ruby, not Puppet!

> When you use a variable name inside a quoted string, it's a good idea to wrap it in curly brackets as follows:
>
> ```
> "The domain is ${site_domain}"
> ```
>
> Not:
>
> ```
> "The domain is $site_domain"
> ```
>
> This helps to distinguish the variable name from the literal string it's used in (and any other variables you might be using in the same string).

Now we can use the template to generate the Nginx virtual host file:

```
file { '/etc/nginx/sites-enabled/cat-pictures.conf':
  content => template('nginx/vhost.conf.erb'),
  notify  => Service['nginx'],
}
```

This looks just like any other `file` resource, with a `content` attribute, but we previously gave the contents of the file as a literal string:

```
content => "Hello, world\n",
```

Instead, here there is a call to the `template` function:

```
content => template('nginx/vhost.conf.erb'),
```

The argument to `template` tells Puppet where to find the template file. The path

```
nginx/vhost.conf.erb
```

Translates to

```
modules/nginx/templates/vhost.conf.erb
```

Puppet now evaluates the template, inserting the values of any variables referenced in `<%= %>` signs, and generates the final output:

```
server {
  listen 80;
  root /var/www/cat-pictures;
  server_name cat-pictures.com;
}
```

You might think this is a lot of trouble to go to just to end up with the same file we had before. Of course, having gone to the trouble of using a template, we can now easily create virtual hosts for other sites using the same template file:

```
node 'demo2' {
  include nginx

  $site_name = 'dog-pictures'
  $site_domain = 'dog-pictures.com'
  file { '/etc/nginx/sites-enabled/dog-pictures.conf':
    content => template('nginx/vhost.conf.erb'),
    notify  => Service['nginx'],
  }
}
```

Inline templates

You don't need to use a separate template file to take advantage of the power of templates.
The `inline_template` function lets you put a template string right in your Puppet code:

```
file { '/tmp/the_answer.txt':
  content => inline_template("What do you get if you multiply six by
nine? <%= 6 * 7 %>.\n")
}
```

System facts

It's often useful to be able to get information about the system, such as its IP address
or operating system version. Puppet's companion tool, **Facter**, provides this information.
To see the list of facts available about your system, run the command:

```
ubuntu@demo:~/puppet$ facter
architecture => amd64
...
uptime_hours => 2109
uptime_seconds => 7593471
virtual => xenu
```

You can reference any of these facts in a template (or in your Puppet code) just like
a variable:

```
content => inline_template("My address is <%= @ipaddress %>.\n")
```

There are a lot of facts. The ones you will most likely use in Puppet manifests are:

- `architecture` – reports the system processor architecture and bitness
  (32- or 64-bit)

- `fqdn` – the fully-qualified domain name of the machine; for example,
  `demo.cat-pictures.com`

- `hostname` – just the hostname part; for example, `demo`

- `ipaddress` – the IP address of the primary or first network interface. If there
  are multiple interfaces, you can find their addresses with `ipaddress_eth0`,
  `ipaddress_eth1`, and so on

- `memorysize` – the amount of physical memory present

- `operatingsystem` – the name of the machine's OS (for example, `Ubuntu`
  or `CentOS`)

- `operatingsystemrelease` – the specific OS version (for example, `12.04`
  for Ubuntu Precise)

Doing the math

Actually, you can do more than just insert variables and facts in templates. Puppet's templating engine is called **ERB**, which uses Ruby, and in fact, everything between the `<%=` and `%>` signs is Ruby code. So you can do math:

```
Two plus two is <%= 2 + 2 %>
```

Or call Ruby methods:

```
The time is <%= Time.now %>
```

Or evaluate Ruby expressions:

```
$vagrant_vm = inline_template("<%= FileTest.exists?('/tmp/vagrant-
puppet') ? 'true' : 'false' %>")
```

Putting it all together

You can combine facts, variables, arithmetic, string operations, and Ruby logic to do some quite sophisticated things in templates. Here's an example that uses the `memorysize` fact to modify a configuration file based on the physical RAM present. Unfortunately for us, `memorysize` isn't returned as a simple integer representing the number of megabytes, say. It's a string that includes the unit, for example `512.20 MB` or `31.40 GB`.

So before we can do computations with this figure, we need to normalize it to an integer number of megabytes:

```
<% raw_memsize = @memorysize
   if raw_memsize.include?("GB")
     mem_in_mb = raw_memsize.to_f * 1024
   else
     mem_in_mb = raw_memsize.to_f
   end
%>
export HADOOP_DATANODE_OPTS="-XX:MaxDirectMemorySize=<%= ( mem_in_mb *
0.25 ).to_i %>M ${HADOOP_DATANODE_OPTS}"
```

Having copied this code (of mine) from a production system, I see that it isn't really very good. It assumes the only units returned will be MB or GB, so it will fail on systems with memory measured in terabytes (TB), for example. But you get the idea, and your code will be better.

Summary

A quick rundown of what we've learned in this chapter.

Exec resources

Anything you can do on the command line, Puppet can do with an `exec` resource.
Specify the command to run using the `command` attribute:

```
exec { 'Run my arbitrary command':
  command => '/bin/echo I ran this command on `/bin/date` >/tmp/
command.output.txt',
}
```

By default, an `exec` resource will always be applied, every time you run Puppet. There are
several ways to control whether or when an `exec` will be applied:

- ♦   `creates` runs the `exec` only if a given file doesn't exist
- ♦   `onlyif` runs the `exec` only if a given command succeeds
- ♦   `unless` runs the `exec` only if a given command fails

To run the command in a specified directory, use the `cwd` attribute:

```
exec { 'Download public key for John':
  cwd      => '/tmp',
  command => '/usr/bin/wget http://bitfieldconsulting.com/files/john.
pub',
  creates => '/tmp/john.pub',
}
```

To apply the command only when triggered by some other resource, use the
`refreshonly` attribute:

```
exec { 'icinga-config-check':
  command      => '/usr/sbin/icinga -v /etc/icinga/icinga.cfg && /usr/
sbin/service icinga restart',
  refreshonly => true,
  subscribe    => File['/etc/icinga/icinga.cfg'],
}
```

This will apply the `exec` only when the resource it subscribes to (/etc/icinga/icinga.
cfg) is changed. You could have the other resource `notify` the `exec` instead, which has the
same effect.

For short sequences of commands, you can chain them in a single `exec` using the `&` shell operator:

```
/usr/sbin/icinga -v /etc/icinga/icinga.cfg && /usr/sbin/service icinga
restart
```

For longer sequences using multiple `exec` resources, you can specify the necessary ordering using `require`:

```
exec { 'command-1':
  command => '/bin/echo Step 1',
}

exec { 'command-2':
  command => '/bin/echo Step 2',
  require => Exec['command-1'],
}
```

Puppet requires you to specify the full path to each command you run in an `exec`, unless you specify a list of paths to search for commands using the `path` attribute:

```
exec { 'Run my arbitrary command':
  command => 'echo I ran this command on `date` >/tmp/command.output.
txt',
  path    => ['/bin', '/usr/bin'],
}
```

You can set a default list of paths for all `exec` resources in your `site.pp` file:

```
Exec {
  path => ['/bin', '/usr/bin'],
}
```

Scheduled jobs

To run commands at a specified time of day, or at regular intervals, you can use a `cron` resource:

```
cron { 'Back up cat-pictures':
  command => '/usr/bin/rsync -az /var/www/cat-pictures/ /cat-pictures-
backup/',
  hour    => '04',
  minute  => '00',
}
```

You can use any combination of these attributes to set the scheduled time for the job: `hour`, `minute`, `day`, `weekday`, `monthday`, `month`.

You can run a job at regular intervals (every 5 minutes, for example) with a setting like this:

```
minute => '*/5',
```

Cron jobs default to running as `root`. To make a job execute as a particular user, specify the `user` attribute:

```
user => 'www-data',
```

Recursive file resources

To have Puppet copy a whole tree of files, use the `recurse` attribute on a `file` resource:

```
file { '/var/www/cat-pictures/img':
  source  => 'puppet:///modules/cat-pictures/img',
  recurse => true,
  require => File['/var/www/cat-pictures'],
}
```

Templates

Templates can be used wherever you need to insert information into a file based on Puppet variables or Facter facts. You can also use Ruby code in templates to do math or string computations, or read and write files, anything, in fact, that Ruby can do. Just specify a template file using the `template` function:

```
file { '/etc/nginx/sites-enabled/cat-pictures.conf':
  content => template('nginx/vhost.conf.erb'),
  notify  => Service['nginx'],
}
```

The most common use for templates is simply inserting the value of a variable:

```
server_name <%= @site_domain %>;
```

But you can use any valid Ruby code in a template:

```
The time is <%= Time.now %>
```

Inline templates don't require a separate template file; you just supply the template to Puppet as a string in your manifest and call the `inline_template` function to evaluate it:

```
file { '/tmp/the_answer.txt':
  content => inline_template("What do you get if you multiply six by
nine? <%= 6 * 7 %>.\n")
}
```

7
Definitions and Classes

*There are basically two types of people. People who accomplish things, and
people who claim to have accomplished things. The first group is less crowded.*

— *Mark Twain*

In this chapter, you'll learn how to group resources into reusable clumps that you can refer
to by name, making it easy to create lots of similar resources at once. You can also make your
Puppet manifests shorter, neater, and more readable by eliminating duplicated code.

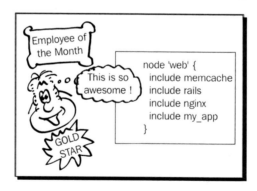

Grouping resources into arrays

Suppose you have several instances of the same resource, as follows:

```
package { 'php5-cli':
  ensure => installed,
}

package { 'php5-fpm':
  ensure => installed,
}

package { 'php-pear':
  ensure => installed,
}
```

You can make your code shorter and simpler by grouping them into a single resource declaration with a list of names, as follows:

```
package { [ 'php5-cli',
            'php5-fpm',
            'php-pear' ]:
  ensure => installed,
}
```

A comma-separated list in square brackets, shown in the following code line, is called an array:

```
[ 'php5-cli', 'php5-fpm', 'php-pear' ]
```

I've split it over multiple lines to make it more readable, but it's all the same to Puppet. Arrays are acceptable in many places where otherwise you might use a single value:

```
require => [ Package['ntp'], File['/etc/ntp.conf'] ],
```

And they are especially useful when declaring lots of instances of the same resource type, which only differ in their names:

```
file { [ '/var/www/myapp',
         '/var/www/myapp/releases',
         '/var/www/myapp/shared',
         '/var/www/myapp/shared/config',
         '/var/www/myapp/shared/log',
         '/var/www/myapp/shared/pids',
         '/var/www/myapp/shared/system' ]:
  ensure => directory,
}
```

Any attributes you add (file ownership or mode, for example) will be the same for every file in the array. This is a great way to set attributes for a large number of resources all at once.

Definitions

Grouping resources into arrays is very helpful, but it only works with instances of a single resource type. What if you want to group resources of different types? Let's take an example: creating scheduled jobs that run a script at a particular time. For each job, we need to have Puppet deploy the script file itself to the server:

```
file { '/usr/local/bin/backup_database':
  source => 'puppet:///modules/scripts/backup_database',
  mode   => '0755',
}
```

We also need to create a `cron` resource to run the script:

```
cron { 'Run backup_database':
  command => '/usr/local/bin/backup_database',
  hour    => '00',
  minute  => '00',
}
```

So far, so good. But when you have ten jobs to run, all this typing gets a little repetitive:

```
file { '/usr/local/bin/job1':
  source => 'puppet:///modules/scripts/job1',
  mode   => '0755',
}
cron { 'Run job1':
  command => '/usr/local/bin/job1',
  hour    => '00',
  minute  => '00',
}
file { '/usr/local/bin/job2':
  source => 'puppet:///modules/scripts/job2',
  mode   => '0755',
}
cron { 'Run job2':
  command => '/usr/local/bin/job2',
  hour    => '00',
  minute  => '00',
}
...
# and so on
```

Worse, when you have lots of duplicated code like this, it becomes very difficult to maintain. If you want to change a parameter for all your jobs (say, to run them all at 1 a.m. instead of midnight) you have to track down every job in your code and make the same modification. That's tedious and error-prone.

A better way is to group this pair of resources (the file and the cron job) and give them a name using the `define` keyword:

```
# Manages a script plus the cron job to run it
define script_job() {
  file { "/usr/local/bin/${name}":
    source => "puppet:///modules/scripts/${name}",
    mode   => '0755',
  }
  cron { "Run ${name}":
    command => "/usr/local/bin/${name}",
    hour    => '00',
    minute  => '00',
  }
}
```

You can see that this is exactly the same as the resources we had before, except that the name of the job has been replaced with `${name}`, and the whole thing is wrapped inside these lines:

```
define script_job() {
  ...
}
```

The resource that you create using the `define` keyword is called a **definition**. A definition can be used just like a regular resource type:

```
script_job { 'backup_database':
}
```

When Puppet sees this, it effectively replaces it with the following:

```
file { '/usr/local/bin/backup_database':
  source => 'puppet:///modules/scripts/backup_database',
  mode   => '0755',
}
cron { 'Run backup_database':
  command => '/usr/local/bin/backup_database',
  hour    => '00',
  minute  => '00',
}
```

Wherever `${name}` occurred in the definition, it's been replaced with `backup_database`.

Passing parameters to definitions

So a definition can encapsulate a bunch of different resources and each of them has access to the $name variable. What if you want to add another variable? For example, in the preceding `script_job` example, you might want to make the `hour` a parameter rather than running all your jobs at midnight.

To do this, add the name of the parameter in round brackets following the name of the define:

```
define script_job( $hour ) {
    ...
}
```

You can then refer to $hour anywhere inside the definition and get its value:

```
cron { "Run ${name}":
  command => "/usr/local/bin/${name}",
  hour    => $hour,
  minute  => '00',
}
```

Quotes

If you put double quotes around a string, Puppet will process it for variable references (replacing `${name}` with `backup_database`, for example). It will also interpret the special escape sequences such as `\n` for new line.

If you use single quotes, Puppet will leave the string just as it is. So Puppet Labs official style guidelines say:

All strings that do not contain variables should be enclosed in single quotes. Double quotes should be used when variable interpolation is required.

When you declare an instance of `script_job`, you now have to pass in a value for `hour` just like any other resource attribute:

```
script_job { 'backup_database':
  hour => '05',
}
```

You can pass more than one parameter using a comma-separated list:

```
define script_job( $hour, $minute ) {
  file { "/usr/local/bin/${name}":
    source => "puppet:///modules/scripts/${name}",
    mode   => '0755',
  }
```

```
cron { "Run ${name}":
  command => "/usr/local/bin/${name}",
  hour    => $hour,
  minute  => $minute,
  }
}
```

And passing multiple parameters to a definition is just like setting multiple attributes on a regular resource:

```
script_job { 'backup_database':
  hour   => '05',
  minute => '30',
}
```

Optional parameters

We don't always care what time a job runs, so it would be nice to have the `hour` and `minute` parameters take some default value (`00`, say). You can do this by specifying the default value in the parameter list:

```
define script_job( $hour = '00', $minute = '00' ) {
  ...
}
```

Now if we don't specify an `hour` or `minute` for a `script_job`, they will get the default values. Here is an instance of `script_job` declared this way, with no parameters:

```
script_job { 'backup_database':
}
```

This results in a job that runs at midnight. However, if you pass in values for `hour` or `minute`, they will override the defaults, and a `script_job` like this will run every hour:

```
script_job { 'download_tweets':
  hour => "*",
}
```

Time for action – creating a definition for Nginx websites

Previously we set up an Nginx for the `cat-pictures.com` site, and created a virtual host template so we could create many websites that differ only in a couple of parameters. Let's extend that a little further, and create a definition that includes everything required for an Nginx website.

Following the success of `cat-pictures.com` and its sister site `dog-pictures.com`, the creative department is building a new site where users can upload cute pictures of all kinds of animals. Your job is to use Puppet to set up a server for the new `adorable-animals.com` site.

1. In your Puppet repo, create the file `modules/nginx/manifests/website.pp` with the following contents:

```
# Manage an Nginx virtual host
define nginx::website( $site_domain ) {
  include nginx
  $site_name = $name
  file { "/etc/nginx/sites-enabled/${site_name}.conf":
    content => template('nginx/vhost.conf.erb'),
    notify  => Service['nginx'],
  }
}
```

2. Modify your `manifests/nodes.pp` file as follows:

```
node 'demo' {
  nginx::website { 'adorable-animals':
    site_domain => 'adorable-animals.com',
  }
}
```

3. Run Puppet:

```
ubuntu@demo:~/puppet$ papply

Notice: /Stage[main]//Node[demo]/Nginx::Website[adorable-animals]/
File[/etc/nginx/sites-enabled/adorable-animals.conf]/ensure:
defined content as '{md5}53febc966302b52afc5346803606ced3'

Notice: /Stage[main]/Nginx/Service[nginx]: Triggered 'refresh'
from 1 events

Notice: Finished catalog run in 0.35 seconds
```

What just happened?

When you include this on your node:

```
nginx::website { 'adorable-animals':
  site_domain => 'adorable-animals.com',
}
```

Puppet looks up the definition of `nginx::website` and finds this:

```
define nginx::website( $site_domain ) {
```

The first step in this definition is:

```
include nginx
```

This pulls in the `nginx` class, which we set up in earlier chapters to manage the Nginx server.

The next line sets up the `$site_name` variable that we're going to use in the template:

```
$site_name = $name
```

You might remember that `$name` is a special parameter that Puppet sets implicitly for you. When you declare a resource, you give it a name in quotes after the resource type:

```
package { 'nginx':
  ...

}
```

So inside that package definition, `$name` will have the value `nginx`. Similarly, we declared this instance of `nginx::website` with the name `adorable-animals`:

```
nginx::website { 'adorable-animals':
```

So here, `$name` will have the value `adorable-animals`. We assign this value to the variable `$site_name`.

Next, we declare a `file` resource for the Nginx virtual host file:

```
file { "/etc/nginx/sites-enabled/${site_name}.conf":
```

We know that `$site_name` has the value `adorable-animals`, so the actual file Puppet creates will be `/etc/nginx/sites-enabled/adorable-animals.conf`.

The contents of this file will be read from a template:

```
content => template('nginx/vhost.conf.erb'),
```

The template file, which we created previously, contains:

```
server {
  listen 80;
  root /var/www/<%= site_name %>;
  server_name <%= site_domain %>;
}
```

Puppet will interpolate the values for `site_name` and `site_domain` into this template, as we saw in the previous chapter. So the actual contents of the file will be:

```
server {
  listen 80;
  root /var/www/adorable-animals;
  server_name adorable-animals.com;
}
```

Multiple instances of definitions

Of course, now that we've made it so easy to set up websites in just a couple of lines of Puppet code, we can make a few more of them:

```
nginx::website { 'adorable-animals-staging':
  site_domain => 'staging.adorable-animals.com',
}
nginx::website { 'amusing-animals':
  site_domain => 'funny.adorable-animals.com',
}
```

Exercise

Extend the `nginx::website` definition so that it restarts or reloads the `nginx` service whenever a virtual host file changes.

Classes

We've seen classes before, when we used the `class` keyword to group together the Puppet resources that implement some particular service, such as Nginx:

```
# Manage nginx webserver
class nginx {
  package { 'nginx':
    ensure => installed,
  }
}
```

Defining classes

The `class` keyword introduces a new class definition:

```
class nginx {
  ...
}
```

You can also specify some parameters that the class accepts:

```
class appserver($domain,$database) {
    ...
}
```

The parameters can take default values, as with a definition:

```
class hadoop($role = 'node') {
    ...
}
```

Putting classes inside modules

It's a good idea to organize your classes into modules, just as we did with the `nginx` class. Each class should be stored in the `modules/MODULE_NAME/manifests` directory, in a file named after the class, with each file containing just one class.

So if we create an `nginx::loadbalancer` class, the definition should look like this:

```
class nginx::loadbalancer {
    ...
}
```

It should go in the file `modules/nginx/manifests/loadbalancer.pp`.

The exception is the class named after the module (for example, `nginx`). This should be in the file `modules/nginx/manifests/init.pp`.

Declaring classes

There are different ways to declare a class (that is, to create an instance of it and apply it to the current node) once you've defined it. If you don't need to give the class parameters, the simplest way is to use `include`, as we did before:

```
include nginx
```

Alternatively, you can use `require`. This behaves just like `include`, except it specifies that everything in the required class must be applied immediately, before Puppet moves on to the next part of the code:

```
require nginx
```

If the class does need parameters, declare it like this (a bit like a resource):

```
class { 'cluster_node':
  role => 'master',
}
```

You can include the same class from several different places, and Puppet won't mind. But you can only use a resource-like declaration once (because resources have to be unique).

What's the difference between a class and a definition?

So far, a class looks much like a definition. What's the difference? Why would you use a class instead of a definition, or vice versa?

Well, there is some overlap between them. Both classes and definitions bundle a group of different resources into a single named entity that you can create instances of, with some optional parameters. In older versions of Puppet, classes didn't take parameters, which made the two types more distinct.

However, there are important differences. Classes are **singletons**; that is, Puppet only allows one instance of a class to exist on a node at a time.

This can be very useful when the class has system-wide effects (installing Nginx, for example) and you want to prevent it from being used multiple times. If you had two Nginx classes, each specifying a different version of Nginx, that could cause problems.

Definitions, by contrast, can have as many instances as you like. We saw this earlier when we created multiple websites on the same machine using the `nginx::website` definition.

So if you're wondering which to use, consider:

◆ Will you need to have multiple instances of this on the same node (for example, a website)? If so, use a **definition**.

◆ Could this cause conflicts with other instances of the same thing on this node (for example, a web server)? If so, use a **class**.

Time for action – creating an NTP class

Let's build an example class that manages the NTP time service. The class will take an optional parameter specifying an NTP server to sync from.

1. First, create the directories for an `ntp` module:

```
ubuntu@demo:~/puppet$ mkdir modules/ntp
ubuntu@demo:~/puppet$ mkdir modules/ntp/manifests
ubuntu@demo:~/puppet$ mkdir modules/ntp/templates
```

2. Create the file `modules/ntp/manifests/init.pp` with the following contents:

```
# Manage NTP server
class ntp($server='UNSET') {
  package { 'ntp':
    ensure => installed,
  }

  file { '/etc/ntp.conf':
    content => template('ntp/ntp.conf.erb'),
    notify  => Service['ntp'],
  }

  service { 'ntp':
    ensure  => running,
    enable  => true,
    require => [ Package['ntp'], File['/etc/ntp.conf'] ],
  }
}
```

3. Create the file `modules/ntp/templates/ntp.conf.erb` with the following contents:

```
driftfile /var/lib/ntp/ntp.drift

<% if server != 'UNSET' -%>
server <%= server %> prefer
<% end -%>
server 0.ubuntu.pool.ntp.org
server 1.ubuntu.pool.ntp.org
server 2.ubuntu.pool.ntp.org
server 3.ubuntu.pool.ntp.org
server ntp.ubuntu.com

restrict -4 default kod notrap nomodify nopeer noquery
restrict -6 default kod notrap nomodify nopeer noquery
restrict 127.0.0.1
restrict ::1
```

4. Modify your `manifests/nodes.pp` as follows:

```
node 'demo' {
  class { 'ntp':
    server => 'us.pool.ntp.org',
  }
}
```

5. Run Puppet:

```
ubuntu@demo:~/puppet$ papply
Notice: /Stage[main]/Ntp/Package[ntp]/ensure: created
Notice: /Stage[main]/Ntp/File[/etc/ntp.conf]/ensure: defined
content as '{md5}65e3b66fbf63d0c6c667179b5d0c5216'
Notice: /Stage[main]/Ntp/Service[ntp]: Triggered 'refresh' from 1
events
Notice: Finished catalog run in 4.99 seconds
```

What just happened?

Let's take a detailed look at the `ntp` class definition. First, we give the class name and its parameters:

```
class ntp($server='UNSET') {
  ...
}
```

The class takes one parameter, `server`, with a default value of UNSET (so the parameter is optional). It's a good idea to set your default values to something like UNSET, which makes it very obvious that a value hasn't been provided, rather than using an empty string.

The class will install the `ntp` package:

```
package { 'ntp':
  ensure => installed,
}
```

We will now set up the configuration file `/etc/ntp.conf`, using a template:

```
file { '/etc/ntp.conf':
  content => template('ntp/ntp.conf.erb'),
  notify  => Service['ntp'],
}
```

The template contains the following logic:

```
<% if server != 'UNSET' -%>
server <%= server %> prefer
<% end -%>
```

This means that if the value of `$server` is UNSET, everything between the `<% if -%>` and `<% end -%>` tags will be ignored, and the file will contain only the default NTP settings.

If `$server` is anything other than UNSET, a line like this will be added to the file:

```
server us.pool.ntp.org prefer
```

Here `us.pool.ntp.org` is the value of `$server` that we passed in to the class.

Finally, we manage the `ntp` service itself:

```
service { 'ntp':
  ensure  => running,
  enable  => true,
  require => [ Package['ntp'], File['/etc/ntp.conf'] ],
}
```

Note that this depends on both the `ntp` package (we can hardly start the service until the software's installed) and the `ntp.conf` file. As we saw in *Chapter 3, Packages, Files, and Services*, `require` implies `notify`, so if the `ntp.conf` file is changed later on, the service will be restarted to pick up the changes.

Summary

A quick rundown of what we've learned in this chapter.

Arrays

You can refer to or declare a number of identical resources concisely by giving them as an **array**:

```
package { [ 'php5-cli', 'php5-fpm', 'php-pear' ]:
  ensure => installed,
}
```

Definitions

You can group together resources of any type by using the `define` keyword to create a **definition**:

```
define script_job() {
  RESOURCE1
  RESOURCE2
  ...
}
```

You create an instance of a definition by declaring it just as though it were a built-in resource:

```
script_job { 'backup_database': }
```

Definitions can take **parameters**, if you specify them in () after the definition name:

define script_job($hour, $minute) {

  ...

}

You can make these parameters **optional** by giving default values for them:

```
define script_job( $hour = '00', $minute = '00' ) {
  ...
}
```

To pass parameters to the definition, specify them just like normal resource attributes:

```
script_job { 'backup_database':
  hour   => '05',
  minute => '30',
}
```

Classes

Classes are like definitions, and you introduce them with the class keyword:

```
class nginx::loadbalancer {
```

If the class takes no parameters, you can use the `include` or `require` keywords to create an instance of the class on a node:

```
include postfix
require loadbalancer::nginx
```

If the class takes parameters, you use the `class` keyword to instantiate it, but in a **resource-like** way:

```
class { 'cluster_node':
  role => 'master',
}
```

You can include or require the same class in many different places without a problem, but if the class takes parameters this isn't the case. There can only be one instance of a parameterized class on each node. This makes parameterized classes more suitable for things that make system-wide changes that could potentially conflict with other instances of the same class.

8

Expressions and Logic

A young man should read five hours in a day, and so may acquire a great deal of knowledge.

— Samuel Johnson

In this chapter, you'll learn how to make choices in your Puppet manifests, how to do arithmetic, logic, and string operations in the Puppet language, and how to use regular expressions to match patterns in strings. You'll also find out about some useful Puppet data types: arrays and hashes.

Conditionals

It's useful to be able to do different things in a manifest depending on the value of some variable or expression. Puppet provides several ways to do this. The first is the `if` statement.

If statements

An `if` statement has the following form:

```
if EXPRESSION {
  OPTIONAL_SOMETHING
}
```

The part of the manifest represented by `OPTIONAL_SOMETHING` will only be applied if the value of `EXPRESSION` is true. We'll learn more about expressions later in the chapter, but for now let's take a simple example:

```
if $eggs == 61 {
   notify { 'Glory be, eggs have just gone up to 61¢ a dozen!': }
}
```

Here the `EXPRESSION` is:

```
$eggs == 61
```

The `==` operator means "is equal to".

> Note the difference between `$eggs == 61` and `$eggs = 61`
>
> `$eggs = 61` has a different meaning to Puppet. The single `=` operator has the effect of assigning the value `61` to the variable `$eggs`, while the double `==` operator tests equality. So in conditional expressions—expressions in an `if` statement, for example—we always use `==`, not `=`.

Puppet reads the expression `$eggs == 61`, and decides whether it evaluates to `true` or `false`. If the variable `$eggs` does have the value `61`, the expression will be true, and if it doesn't, it will be false.

If the expression is true, Puppet will apply everything inside the braces:

```
notify { 'Glory be, eggs have just gone up to 61¢ a dozen!': }
```

If the expression is false, Puppet will simply skip the contents of the braces and proceed to the next part of the manifest. So `if` is called a conditional statement; it makes part of the manifest conditional on some expression being true.

else and elsif

You can extend the `if` statement by using `else`:

```
if $::operatingsystem == 'zx81' {
  notify { 'Enabling experimental Puppet ZX81 support': }
} else {
  notify { 'ZX81 not detected': }
}
```

The contents of the `else` branch will only be applied if the condition is not true.

To build up more complex conditional statements, you can use `elsif` to add more tests. Puppet will try them in sequence:

```
if $::processorcount >= 16 {
  include cpu_intensive_application
} elsif $::processorcount >= 4 {
  include medium_application
} else {
  include lightweight_application
}
```

As you can see, the extended form of the `if` statement looks like this:

```
if EXPRESSION {
  OPTIONAL_SOMETHING
} elsif ANOTHER_EXPRESSION {
  OPTIONAL_SOMETHING_ELSE
} else {
  OPTIONAL_OTHER_THING
}
```

You can have as many `elsif` branches as you want; Puppet will test each of the conditions in order, and if none of them matches the `else` branch (if there is one) will be applied instead.

Unless statements

As you might imagine, `unless` is like `if`, but with the opposite sense. The block is not applied if the expression is true. An `unless` statement has this form:

```
unless EXPRESSION {
  OPTIONAL_SOMETHING
}
```

Again, EXPRESSION is a logical expression (one that can evaluate to true or false). This time, the OPTIONAL_SOMETHING is only applied if EXPRESSION is false.

You can't use `elsif` or `else` with `unless`; Puppet treats this as a syntax error.

Case statements

If you just have one or two choices to make, the `if` statement is ideal. However, if you need to choose between several alternatives, it becomes awkward to write:

```
if $::operatingsystem == 'Ubuntu' {
  include os_specific::ubuntu
```

```
    } elsif $::operatingsystem == 'Debian' {
      include os_specific::debian
    } elsif $::operatingsystem == 'RedHat' {
      include os_specific::redhat
    } else {
      include os_specific::default
    }
```

For situations like this, Puppet provides the `case` statement:

```
  case $::operatingsystem {
    'Ubuntu': { include os_specific::ubuntu }
    'Debian': { include os_specific::debian }
    'RedHat': { include os_specific::redhat }
    default : { include os_specific::default }
  }
```

`case` takes an expression and tries to match it against a list of values (the cases). If one matches, Puppet will apply the corresponding code block. If there is a `default` case, this will be applied if none of the other cases match.

The general form of a `case` statement is:

```
  case EXPRESSION {
    CASE1 { BLOCK1 }
    CASE2 { BLOCK2 }
    CASE3 { BLOCK3 }
    ...
    default : { ... }
  }
```

Note that `EXPRESSION` can be any expression; it's not restricted to logical expressions as the `if` and `unless` statements are.

The code blocks `BLOCK1`, `BLOCK2`, and `BLOCK3` can be any Puppet code, though it's a good idea to keep the blocks short enough so that you can see the whole case statement at once. If you need to have a lot of code in the blocks, you can use `include` to apply classes you've defined somewhere else.

Puppet will apply only the first case that matches, and ignore any subsequent ones, so if it's possible for there to be multiple matches you should list them in order of preference. The `default` case must always come at the end.

The default case

It's good practice to always have a default case. If your case statement is supposed to always match something, then you can have the default case signal an error using the fail function:

```
default: { fail('This should never happen') }
```

This will halt Puppet with the error message you specify.

Alternatively, you can provide an empty code block to default:

```
default: { }
```

This makes it clear to anyone reading your code that no action is needed if none of the cases match. It's a good principle of programming that "explicit is better than implicit."

Matching multiple cases

You can specify two or more cases that will trigger the same code block by separating the values with commas as shown in the following code snippet:

```
case $::operatingsystem {
  'Debian', 'Ubuntu': {
    include os_specific::debianlike
  }
}
```

Selectors

Sometimes you want to choose between a number of different values depending on the result of some expression. You could do it with a case statement that sets a variable:

```
case $::operatingsystem {
  'Ubuntu': {
    $os_type = 'Debianlike'
  }
  'RedHat': {
    $os_type = 'Redhatlike'
  }
  'Darwin': {
    $os_type = 'Mac OS'
  }
  default: {
    $os_type = 'UNKNOWN'
  }
}
notify { "You're running a ${os_type} system": }
```

But this is a bit tedious and repetitive. For situations like this, Puppet provides the **selector**, which is like a `case` statement, but instead of matching a case and applying a code block, it matches a case and returns a value.

```
$os_type = $::operatingsystem ? {
  'Ubuntu' => 'Debianlike',
  'RedHat' => 'Redhatlike',
  'Darwin' => 'Mac OS',
  default  => 'UNKNOWN',
}
notify { "You're running a ${os_type} system": }
```

As with a `case` statement, Puppet goes through the list in order, returning the first match it finds. If nothing matches, the value for `default` is returned.

You can use a selector anywhere that expects a value, but it's good style to assign the value of a selector to a variable, and then use that variable, as in the `$os_type` example.

Expressions

It's time to look at expressions in a little more detail, and see what kind of expressions Puppet allows us to construct.

Comparisons

An important kind of expression is the **comparison expression**. This compares two values, and the expression is true or false depending on the result of the comparison.

Equality

We've already seen an expression involving a comparison of two values:

```
$eggs == '61'
```

And we know the `==` operator means "is equal to." Its opposite is the `!= operator` (not equal to):

```
$username != 'FOTHERINGTON-THOMAS'
```

Comparison expressions like these are **logical** expressions; their value is either true or false. By the way, `true` and `false` are reserved words in Puppet that stand for these logical values. You can use them like any other literal values:

```
$raining = true
if $raining {
  include umbrella
}
```

Magnitude

You can also compare values using the following operators:

- ◆ > (greater than)
- ◆ < (less than)
- ◆ >= (greater than or equal to)
- ◆ <= (less than or equal to)

Expressions with these operators are also logical expressions:

```
if $eggs >= 61 {
   notify { 'YOU KNOW I GOT NO SENSE OF EGGS': }
}
```

However, their **operands** (the values they work on) can only be numbers. If you try to say something as follows:

```
if $eggs > 'TALBOT?' {
   ...
}
```

Puppet will not self-destruct like a computer in a bad sci-fi movie, but it will complain:

Error: comparison of Fixnum with String failed

Substrings

Similarly, there is another comparison operator that only works with string operands, in.

```
if 'eggs' in 'Can you believe the price of eggs?' {
   ...
}
```

in tests whether the first operand is a substring of the other. For example, this expression is true:

```
'spring' in 'springfield'
```

But this expression is false:

```
'Paris' in 'the spring'
```

Boolean operators

Boolean, or logical, operators work on logical values (things that evaluate to true or false). You can use them to build up more complex expressions from simpler components. For example, the and operator takes two logical expressions as operands:

```
$eggs > 61 and $eggs < 100
```

This expression is true if both operands are true. So the expression will be true if $eggs is both greater than 61 and less than 100.

If one or both of the operands is false, the and expression will also be false.

```
$eggs > 61 and $eggs < 100
```

The preceding expression will be false if $eggs is 120. Although $eggs > 61 is true, $eggs < 100 is false, so the and expression evaluates to false.

The or operator is a little more forgiving. It is true if either (or both) of its operands is true:

```
$eggs > 61 or $today == 'Thursday'
```

The ! (**not**) operator takes only one operand, and flips its value. If $raining is true, then ! $raining is false, and vice versa.

Combining Boolean operators

You can combine Boolean operators, but it's helpful to use parentheses to group different subexpressions together. This makes it clear to you, to Puppet, and to anyone else reading the code what's intended. For example:

```
$today == 'Thursday' and ($eggs < 61 or $eggs > 100)
```

The preceding expression is not the same as this:

```
($today == 'Thursday' and $eggs < 61) or $eggs > 100
```

Arithmetic operators

Puppet's **arithmetic** operators all work with numeric operands, and the value of an arithmetic expression is always a number (so you can't use it as a test in a conditional statement, for example). You can use the following familiar operators:

- ◆ + (addition)
- ◆ - (subtraction)
- ◆ * (multiplication)
- ◆ / (division)

You can combine these operators in any way you like:

```
$celsius = ($fahrenheit - 32) * 5 / 9
```

There are also two **bitwise shift** operators, `<<` and `>>`, which multiply and divide integers by powers of 2.

```
$x << $y
```

The preceding expression multiplies `$x` by 2 to the power of `$y`. So `$x = 1 << 3` evaluates to 1 times 2 cubed, which is 8.

Regular expressions

We've seen a couple of different ways of testing string values already. You can compare strings for equality:

```
if $role == 'webserver' {
    ...
}
```

You can also test whether one string is a substring of another:

```
if 'dunk' in 'doughnuts' {
    ...
}
```

But what if you want to test for patterns of characters? Say, `app` followed by any characters, followed by `staging`. Puppet has a special pattern-matching language you can use for this:

```
if $::hostname =~ /app.*staging/ {
    ...
}
```

This expression will be true if `$::hostname` is any of the following, and many more:

◆ `app_staging`
◆ `app-1-staging`
◆ `application_staging`
◆ `appstaging`
◆ `my_app_staging_server`

Note the slash characters surrounding the pattern:

```
/app.*staging/
```

This kind of pattern is called a **regular expression**, or **regex** for short, and Puppet uses the slash character (/) to mark the start and end of regular expressions.

Operators

The operator which tests whether a string matches a regex, as in the previous example, is the **regex match** operator, `=~`:

```
VALUE =~ /REGEX/
```

The operator with the opposite sense is the **regex non-match** operator, `!~`:

```
VALUE !~ /REGEX/
```

Syntax

The simplest regular expression is just the literal string that you want to match:

```
$animal =~ /cat/
```

Wildcards (which match any single character) are represented by a dot:

```
/c.t/
```

The preceding expression matches `cat`, `cot`, `cut`, `crt`, and so on. To match from zero to any number of wildcard characters, use `.*`:

```
/c.*t/
```

The preceding expression matches `ct`, `cat`, `count`, `constitutionalist`, and so on. To match digits only, use the sequence `\d`:

```
/app\d*/
```

The preceding expression matches `app`, `app1`, `app200`, `app99999`, and so on.

The particular flavor of regular expression language that Puppet recognizes is the same as that implemented by Ruby, so any valid Ruby regex is just fine with Puppet. You can find a good introduction to Ruby regular expression syntax here: `http://www.tutorialspoint.com/ruby/ruby_regular_expressions.htm`

Conditionals

As we've seen, expressions involving regexes are very useful as the test in a conditional statement:

```
if VALUE =~ /REGEX/ {
  DO_SOMETHING
}
```

So you can use regular expressions with `if` and `unless` statements, but you can also use them as cases in `case` statements:

```
case $::ec2_placement_availability_zone {
  /us-.*/: { notify { 'In United States': } }
  /eu-.*/: { notify { 'In Europe': } }
  default: { notify { 'Some other region': } }
}
```

A regular expression can also be a case in a selector:

```
$ec2_family = $::ec2_instance_type ? {
  /t1/     => 'micro',
  /m1/     => 'first generation',
  /m2/     => 'high-memory',
  /m3/     => 'second generation',
  /c1/     => 'high-cpu',
  default => 'other',
}
```

Capture variables

If you need to refer to the actual text that was matched, it will be available in the special variable called $0. This is called a **capture variable**. Within the scope of the conditional statement, you can refer to $0 to get the string that the regex successfully matched, if any:

```
$uname = generate('/bin/uname','-a')
if $uname =~ /\d+\.\d+\.\d+/ {
  notify { "I have kernel version ${0}": }
}
```

The output of the command `uname -a` on a Linux server usually looks something like this:

```
Linux demo 3.2.0-29-virtual #46-Ubuntu SMP Fri Jul 27 17:23:50 UTC 2012
x86_64 x86_64 x86_64 GNU/Linux
```

So the code above looks for a string that matches the regular expression:

```
/\d+\.\d+\.\d+/
```

This expression matches three numbers separated by periods. In this case the match text will be:

```
3.2.0
```

So the output is:

```
Notice: I have kernel version 3.2.0
```

You can also capture smaller parts of the regular expression, by putting it in parentheses, like this:

```
/abc(def)ghi/
```

The value of anything matched by the characters in parentheses will be available as $1:

```
$uname = generate('/bin/uname','-a')
if $uname =~ /(\d+)\.\d+\.\d+/ {
  notify { "I have kernel version ${0}, major version ${1}": }
}

Notice: I have kernel version 3.2.0, major version 3
```

You can use more than one set of parentheses, and the values for each will be available as $1, $2, and so on.

These capture variables are only good within the block of the conditional expression, so use them or lose them. If you need to preserve one of these values for later, you can assign it to a regular variable:

```
if $uname =~ /(\d+)\.\d+\.\d+/ {
  $major_version = $1
}
```

Substitutions

Sometimes it's handy to be able to search and replace text within strings. Puppet gives you this capability with the `regsubst` function, which matches text with a regular expression and replaces it with the value you specify:

```
regsubst(STRING, REGEX, REPLACEMENT)
```

The STRING argument is the input. The REGEX is what you want to match in the input. The REPLACEMENT is what you want to replace any matched text with. For example:

```
$output = regsubst('Look at my cat picture', 'cat', 'dog')
notify { $output: }
```

The output from the preceding code snippet will be:

`Notice: Look at my dog picture`

The regex can simply be a literal string, as in this example, or it can be more complicated:

```
$output = regsubst('Look at my cat picture','my .* picture','something
more interesting')
notify { $output: }
```

The output from the preceding code snippet will be:

`Notice: Look at something more interesting`

You can also use capture variables, as in conditional statements. Here, the contents of successive capture variables are named \1, \2, and so on.

```
$output = regsubst('Look at my cat picture','my (.*) picture','this
adorable \1')
notify { $output: }
```

The output from the preceding code snippet will be:

`Notice: Look at this adorable cat`

 There are a few syntax differences when using regular expressions with regsubst. Instead of putting the regular expression within slashes (/REGEX/) you use quotes ('REGEX'). And as we just saw, the capture variables are named \1, \2, \3 instead of $1, $2, $3. The makers of Puppet put these little differences in to make sure you're paying attention.

Node definitions

A handy place to use regular expressions is in node definitions. You can apply a node definition not merely to a hostname:

```
node 'demo' {
   ...
}
```

Or to a list of hostnames:

```
node 'demo1', 'demo2', 'demo3' {
  ...
}
```

You can also apply a node definition to hostnames matching a regular expression:

```
node /demo.*/ {
  ...
}
```

This is very useful when you have a number of otherwise identical servers whose hostnames match some pattern:

```
node /web.*/ {
   include webserver
}

node /app.*/ {
   include appserver
}

node /db.*/ {
   include dbserver
}
```

> Node definitions don't support capture variables, so you can't capture the matched text and use it inside the node definition as you can in a conditional statement. If you want to capture some part of the hostname, you can do this with `regsubst` and the `$::hostname` fact.

Arrays and hashes

So far we've dealt mostly with strings and numbers, but Puppet has a couple of other data types you can use, which are ways of grouping values together: **arrays** and **hashes**.

Grouping resources with arrays

We've encountered arrays before, when we used them to concisely declare several similar resources:

```
package { [ 'php5-cli', 'php5-fpm', 'php-pear' ]:
  ensure => installed,
}
```

To make an array, all you need to do is put square brackets round it:

```
['jerry', 'george', 'elaine']
```

If you use an array in the context where a resource name is expected, this has the effect of declaring a resource for each member of the array:

```
$developers = ['jerry', 'george', 'elaine']
notify { $developers: }
```

The output from the preceding code snippet will be:

```
Notice: george
Notice: jerry
Notice: elaine
```

This is why the trick of declaring an array of package names works: it declares a `package` resource for each member of the array.

However, this doesn't work if the array is interpolated into a string. In that case, the members of the array are all simply clumped together in the string:

```
$developers = ['jerry', 'george', 'elaine']
notify { "The developers are: $developers": }
```

The output from the preceding code snippet will be:

```
Notice: The developers are: jerrygeorgeelaine
```

Getting values out of arrays

To retrieve a specific element of an array (for example, the first element), put the element number in square brackets after the array name:

```
$developers[0]
```

The elements are numbered from 0 upwards, with 0 being the first element, 1 the second, and so on. If this seems odd to you, you can always refer to element 0 as the zeroth element instead. Computer scientists and mathematicians will understand you perfectly.

You can also number elements backwards from the end of the array. For example, the last element of an array is element `[-1]`:

```
$developers = ['jerry', 'george', 'elaine']
notify { "The last developer is: ${developers[-1]}": }
```

The output from the preceding code snippet will be:

```
Notice: The last developer is: elaine
```

The second-to-last element is [-2], and so on.

You can also use the in operator to test if some value is a member of an array:

```
if $crewmember in ['Frank', 'Dave'] {
  notify { "I'm sorry, ${crewmember}. I'm afraid I can't do that.": }
}
```

Hashes

A hash is a set of pairs of elements. The first member of each pair is called the **key**, and the second is the **value**. Here's an example:

```
$interfaces = {
  'lo0'  => '127.0.0.1',
  'eth0' => '192.168.0.1',
}
```

You can think of a hash as being like an array, but instead of looking up elements by number, you look them up by name (the key):

```
$address = $interfaces['eth0']
notify { "Interface eth0 has address ${address}": }
```

The output from the preceding code snippet will be:

```
Notice: Interface eth0 has address 192.168.0.1
```

The key must be a string, but the value can be any data type:

```
$contrived_example = {
  'fish'   => 'babel',
  'answer' => 42,
  'crew'   => ['Ford Prefect', 'Arthur Dent'],
  'hash'   => { 'Warning' => 'Beware of the leopard' }
}
```

Multilevel hashes

As you can see, the value can be a string, a number, an array, or even another hash. This means you can construct **multilevel** hashes, where you use a series of increasingly specific keys to get what you want. For example:

```
$interfaces = {
  'lo0'  => {
    'address' => '127.0.0.1',
    'netmask' => '255.0.0.0',
  },
  'eth0' => {
    'address' => '192.168.0.1',
    'netmask' => '255.255.255.0',
  }
}
$eth0_netmask = $interfaces['eth0']['netmask']
notify { "eth0 has netmask ${eth0_netmask}": }
```

The output from the preceding code snippet will be:

```
Notice: eth0 has netmask 255.255.255.0
```

Note the syntax for looking up keys in a multilevel hash:

```
$interfaces['eth0']['netmask']
```

Testing hash keys

The in operator also works with hashes, and tests whether the hash has a certain key:

```
if 'eth0' in $interfaces {
  ...
}
```

Summary

A quick rundown of what we've learned in this chapter.

Conditionals

You can conditionally apply a block of Puppet code using an if statement:

```
if EXPRESSION {
  OPTIONAL_SOMETHING
}
```

You can add extra elsif clauses and an optional else clause:

```
if EXPRESSION {
  OPTIONAL_SOMETHING
} elsif ANOTHER_EXPRESSION {
```

```
      OPTIONAL_SOMETHING_ELSE
} else {
    OPTIONAL_OTHER_THING
}
```

The `else` clause, if present, will be applied if none of the conditions match.

The `case` statement lets you conditionally apply code if any of a number of possible cases are matched:

```
case EXPRESSION {
    CASE1 { BLOCK1 }
    CASE2 { BLOCK2 }
    CASE3 { BLOCK3 }
    ...
    default : { ... }
}
```

With a `selector`, you can test a number of cases and return a value:

```
$result = EXPRESSION ? {
    CASE1    => VALUE1,
    CASE2    => VALUE2,
    CASE3    => VALUE3,
    default => DEFAULT_VALUE,
}
```

Operators

You can build expressions using different kinds of operators:

- ◆ Comparison operators (==, !=, <, <=, >, >=)
- ◆ Boolean operators (and, or, !)
- ◆ String, array, or hash membership operators (in)
- ◆ Arithmetic operators (+, -, *, /, <<, >>)

Regular expressions

You can use **regular** expressions to match patterns of characters:

```
if $::hostname =~ /app.*staging/ {
```

Regular expressions can also be the cases for selectors and `case` statements:

```
case $::ec2_placement_availability_zone {
  /us-.*/: { notify { 'In United States': } }
  ...
}


$ec2_family = $::ec2_instance_type ? {
  /t1/     => 'micro',
  ...
}
```

The text matched by a regular expression, or part of a regular expression grouped with parentheses, is available in the **capture** variables `$0`, `$1`, `$2`, and so on.

```
if $uname =~ /(\d+)\.\d+\.\d+/ {
  notify { "I have kernel version ${0}, major version ${1}": }
}
```

Text substitution

To substitute text in strings, use the `regsubst` function with a suitable regular expression:

```
$output = regsubst('Look at my cat picture','my (.*) picture','this adorable \1')
notify { $output: }
```

The output from the preceding code snippet will be:

Notice: Look at this adorable cat

Regular expressions can also be used to match **node definitions**:

```
node /web.*/ {
  include webserver
}
```

Arrays

Arrays are sets of values surrounded by square brackets:

```
['jerry', 'george', 'elaine']
```

You can often use an array in place of a single value:

```
package { [ 'php5-cli', 'php5-fpm', 'php-pear' ]:
  ensure => installed,
}
```

To look up an element in an array by number (starting from zero), use square brackets after the array name:

```
$developers[0]
```

Hashes

A **hash** is a set of key/value pairs grouped inside curly braces:

```
$interfaces = {
  'lo0'  => '127.0.0.1',
  'eth0' => '192.168.0.1',
}
```

You look up hash values with a string key in square brackets after the hash name:

```
$address = $interfaces['eth0']
```

Hash keys must be strings, but hash values can be strings, numbers, arrays, or other hashes:

```
$interfaces = {
  'lo0'  => {
    'address' => '127.0.0.1',
    'netmask' => '255.0.0.0',
  },
  'eth0' => {
    'address' => '192.168.0.1',
    'netmask' => '255.255.255.0',
  }
}
```

To look up a value in a **multilevel hash**, use consecutive keys in square brackets:

```
$interfaces['eth0']['netmask']
```

9

Reporting and troubleshooting

Often, the most important piece of information is that something has gone wrong.

— *Frank Herbert, "God Emperor of Dune"*

In this chapter, you'll learn how to get information on what Puppet's doing, when it runs, the changes it makes, how to monitor Puppet, and what to do about many common errors you may encounter.

Reporting

Most of the time you'll probably be happy for Puppet to just run and do its job. In some situations, however, it can be very useful to have Puppet record information about exactly what it did and when it did it. This facility in Puppet is called **reporting**.

For example, if something is not working as you expected, you can look at Puppet's reports and get a very detailed picture of what's going on. Or you might want to monitor what Puppet is doing across your whole network and record performance information over time. You can also see if Puppet runs are failing, and diagnose the reason.

Summary reports

You can get a quick overview of what Puppet is doing on a given run by using the `--summarize` flag to `puppet apply`. It will report some overall statistics on timing and resources changed:

```
ubuntu@demo:~/puppet$ papply --summarize
Notice: /Stage[main]//Node[demo]/File[/tmp/test]/ensure: defined content
as '{md5}5d41402abc4b2a76b9719d911017c592'
Notice: Finished catalog run in 0.06 seconds
Changes:
            Total: 1
Events:
          Success: 1
            Total: 1
Resources:
          Changed: 1
      Out of sync: 1
          Skipped: 6
            Total: 9
Time:
       Filebucket: 0.00
             File: 0.00
  Config retrieval: 0.15
            Total: 0.16
         Last run: 1360157807
Version:
           Config: 1360157805
           Puppet: 3.0.2
```

This can be helpful if you want to make sure that Puppet is doing what you think it should. However, if you need more information, especially about changes to specific resources, you'll need to enable full reports. We'll see how to do this in the next section.

Enabling reports

Reporting is enabled in the Ubuntu Puppet package by default, but if you're using another distribution or installing Puppet from another source, this may not be the case. To check your setting, run the following command:

```
ubuntu@demo:~/puppet$ sudo puppet config print report
true
```

If the setting is `false`, and you want to enable reporting, edit the file `/etc/puppet/puppet.conf` and add the following setting:

```
[main]
report=true
```

What's in a report?

Puppet produces detailed reports every time it runs, recording the following:

- The date and time of the run
- How long the run took
- The version of Puppet
- Whether the run failed, changed resources, or left them unchanged
- How many resources were changed (if any)
- Every resource in the catalog (the set of resources that apply to this node), with the following information:
    - The name of the resource
    - The resource type
    - Whether or not the resource was out of sync (didn't match the manifest)
    - Whether or not the resource was changed
    - The number of properties (attribute values) that were out of sync
    - The number of properties that were changed
    - If any properties of a resource were changed, the report includes:

        The name of the changed property

        The previous value

        The new value

Let's look at an example. We'll have Puppet make a change to a resource, and then examine the resulting report.

Time for action – generating a report

1. Check whether reporting is enabled:

   ```
   ubuntu@demo:~/puppet$ sudo puppet config print report
   true
   ```

2. If the result is `false`, follow the instructions in the *Enabling reports* section.

3. Edit your `manifests/nodes.pp` file as follows:

   ```
   node 'demo' {
     file { '/tmp/test':
       content => 'Zaphod Beeblebrox, this is a very large drink',
     }
   }
   ```

4. Run Puppet:

   ```
   ubuntu@demo:~/puppet$ papply
   ```

   ```
   Notice: /Stage[main]//Node[demo]/File[/tmp/test]/content: content
   changed '{md5}e705c4d685bf03258eb5ba0dc767905b' to '{md5}
   aea5a3708af83f6e53b4b391b469ae44'
   ```

   ```
   Notice: Finished catalog run in 0.11 seconds
   ```

5. Find the report file generated by Puppet. First, check where Puppet is configured to write its reports (the default location on Ubuntu is `/var/lib/puppet/reports`):

   ```
   ubuntu@demo:~/puppet$ sudo puppet config print reportdir
   /var/lib/puppet/reports
   ```

6. You will need root privileges to read the report:

   ```
   ubuntu@demo:~/puppet$ sudo su -
   root@demo:~#
   ```

7. Change to the report directory:

   ```
   root@demo:~# cd /var/lib/puppet/reports
   ```

8. You should see a directory with the same name as the hostname of your machine:

   ```
   root@demo:/var/lib/puppet/reports# ls
   demo.compute-1.internal
   ```

9. Change to this directory:

```
root@demo:/var/lib/puppet/reports# cd demo.compute-1.internal/
```

10. Check for the most recently created file:

```
root@demo:/var/lib/puppet/reports/demo.compute-1.internal# ls -lt
|head -2
total 1084

-rw-r----- 1 root root   6742 Feb  1 13:43 201302011343.yaml
```

11. The file's name is generated from the date and time of the Puppet run, so the name of your file will be different. Display the contents of the file:

```
root@demo:/var/lib/puppet/reports/demo.compute-1.internal# less
201302011343.yaml
--- !ruby/object:Puppet::Transaction::Report
  status: changed
  kind: apply
  host: demo.compute-1.internal
  configuration_version: 1359726210

  ...
```

12. Look for the section relating to the `file` resource you created:

```
    File[/tmp/test]: !ruby/object:Puppet::Resource::Status
      resource: File[/tmp/test]
      file: /home/ubuntu/puppet/manifests/nodes.pp
      line: 4
      evaluation_time: 0.016333
      change_count: 1
      out_of_sync_count: 1
      tags:
        - file
        - node
        - demo
        - class
      time: 2013-02-01 13:43:32.529725 +00:00
      events:
        - !ruby/object:Puppet::Transaction::Event
          audited: false
```

```
        property: ensure
        previous_value: !ruby/sym absent
        desired_value: !ruby/sym file
        historical_value:
        message: "defined content as '{md5}
   aea5a3708af83f6e53b4b391b469ae44'"
        name: !ruby/sym file_created
        status: success
        time: 2013-02-01 13:43:32.530130 +00:00
   out_of_sync: true
   changed: true
   resource_type: File
   title: /tmp/test
   skipped: false
   failed: false
```

What just happened?

We'll examine this report in detail to see what information Puppet has recorded about what it did.

There will be lots of information in the report, about all the other resources on the machine, as well as some of Puppet's internal data. However, the part we're interested in at the moment is the `Puppet::Resource::Status` section relating to the `/tmp/test` file:

```
File[/tmp/test]: !ruby/object:Puppet::Resource::Status
    resource: File[/tmp/test]
    file: /home/ubuntu/puppet/manifests/nodes.pp
    line: 4
    evaluation_time: 0.016333
    change_count: 1
    out_of_sync_count: 1
```

This section gives the name and type of the resource:

```
    resource: File[/tmp/test]
```

The manifest file and line number where it's defined:

```
    file: /home/ubuntu/puppet/manifests/nodes.pp
    line: 4
```

The time it took to compile the resource definition:

```
evaluation_time: 0.016333
```

The number of properties of the resource that were changed:

```
change_count: 1
```

The number of properties that were found to be out of sync with the manifest:

```
out_of_sync_count: 1
```

There's a `Puppet::Transaction::Event` section for each property that was changed, in this case, only one.

```
- !ruby/object:Puppet::Transaction::Event
  audited: false
  property: ensure
  previous_value: !ruby/sym absent
  desired_value: !ruby/sym file
  historical_value:
  message: "defined content as '{md5}
aea5a3708af83f6e53b4b391b469ae44'"
  name: !ruby/sym file_created
  status: success
  time: 2013-02-01 13:43:32.530130 +00:00
```

This section tells us which property was changed:

```
property: ensure
```

Its previous value:

```
previous_value: !ruby/sym absent
```

The value requested by the manifest (although we didn't specify `ensure => file`, this is implicit for a `file` resource):

```
desired_value: !ruby/sym file
```

Whether the property change was successful:

```
status: success
```

The time the change was made:

```
time: 2013-02-01 13:43:32.530130 +00:00
```

Finally, the `Puppet::Transaction::Report` section provides general data about the Puppet run:

```
--- !ruby/object:Puppet::Transaction::Report
  status: changed
  kind: apply
  host: demo.compute-1.internal
  configuration_version: 1359726210
```

The `status` field indicates that the configuration of the machine was changed on this Puppet run. If the Puppet run was successful, but no resources were changed, the status would be `unchanged`. If there was an error, the status would be `failed`.

Using reports

Although you don't often need to see this level of detail about what Puppet's doing, it can be useful when something's not working right and you need to figure out why.

For example, if you think Puppet should be making a particular change, and it's not happening, you can use the report to help troubleshoot the problem. Turn on reporting, run Puppet, and inspect the report as we did in the previous example. Find the resource in question and you'll be able to see what Puppet thinks it should be, whether it's in sync with the manifest, and whether there were any failures.

For larger-scale reporting on a whole network of Puppet-managed machines, you can set up a report server where Puppet will send reports from each machine. These can then be aggregated and processed, and you can see graphs and results using a tool like Puppet Dashboard. This is beyond the scope of this book, but you can find out more at:

```
https://puppetlabs.com/puppet/related-projects/dashboard/
```

Debug runs

Running Puppet with the `--debug` flag will not produce as much detail as a report, but still gives you much more information than a normal Puppet run. For example:

```
ubuntu@demo:~/puppet$ papply --debug
Debug: importing '/home/ubuntu/puppet/manifests/nodes.pp' in environment
production
Debug: Failed to load library 'selinux' for feature 'selinux'
Debug: Creating default schedules
Debug: Using settings: adding file resource 'graphdir': 'File[/var/lib/
puppet/state/graphs]
:links=>:follow, :backup=>false, :ensure=>:directory, :loglevel=>:debug,
:path=>"/var/lib/puppet/state/graphs"}'
```

```
...
```

Notice: Finished catalog run in 0.08 seconds

Debug: Using settings: adding file resource 'rrddir': 'File[/var/
lib/puppet/rrd]{:links=>:follow, :group=>"puppet", :backup=>false,
:ensure=>:directory, :owner=>"puppet", :mode=>"750", :loglevel=>:debug,
:path=>"/var/lib/puppet/rrd"}'

Debug: Finishing transaction 69968312591020

Debug: Received report to process from demo.compute-1.internal

Debug: Processing report from demo.compute-1.internal with processor
Puppet::Reports::Store

Because the `--debug` flag tells Puppet to output everything it does, this usually produces a lot of information that isn't interesting, but it may help you in some situations to figure out why Puppet is doing something it shouldn't, or not doing something it should.

Noop runs

By its very nature, Puppet can produce big changes on a machine in a single run. Depending on the manifest, it can change or delete files, restart services, drop databases, or do many other potentially destructive things. So it would be nice to have Puppet tell us what it's going to do before it does it.

The `--noop` flag does exactly this. **Noop** stands for **no-operation**; in other words, do everything except actually make changes to the system. This is also sometimes known as **dry-run mode**. Let's see an example:

ubuntu@demo:~/puppet$ papply --noop

Notice: /Stage[main]//Node[demo]/File[/tmp/test]/ensure: current_value
absent, should be file (noop)

Notice: Node[demo]: Would have triggered 'refresh' from 1 events

Notice: Class[Main]: Would have triggered 'refresh' from 1 events

Notice: Stage[main]: Would have triggered 'refresh' from 1 events

Notice: Finished catalog run in 0.06 seconds

This is telling us that Puppet has found one resource out of sync:

Notice: /Stage[main]//Node[demo]/File[/tmp/test]/ensure: current_value
absent, should be file (noop)

The `ensure` property for the file `/tmp/test` should be `file`, but instead it is `absent`. In other words, the manifest says there should be a file `/tmp/test`, but there isn't. Puppet will fix this by creating the file, when you run Puppet without the `--noop` flag.

```
ubuntu@demo:~/puppet$ papply

Notice: /Stage[main]//Node[demo]/File[/tmp/test]/ensure: defined content
as '{md5}aea5a3708af83f6e53b4b391b469ae44'

Notice: Finished catalog run in 0.06 seconds
```

So dry-run mode is very useful for making sure that Puppet will only make the changes you expected to see. If you're not sure what would change, or you want to make sure that your changes won't affect a running service, for example, you can use dry-run mode to find out.

> Be warned: dry-run mode doesn't come with any guarantees. It's quite possible to do a dry run with no errors, but then encounter a problem running Puppet for real. For example, if the manifest tries to install a package that doesn't exist in the repository, this will succeed in dry-run mode, because there's no way for Puppet to know in advance that it won't work. Similarly, `exec` resources won't actually be run, so dry-run mode can't tell you whether they will succeed or fail. Test your critical changes in a staging environment, rather than relying solely on dry-run mode.

Syntax checking

If you want to make sure there are no syntax errors in your manifest, you can use Puppet's `parser validate` command to check this:

```
ubuntu@demo:~/puppet$ puppet parser validate manifests/nodes.pp

Error: Could not parse for environment production: Syntax error at
'server'; expected '}' at /home/ubuntu/puppet/manifests/nodes.pp:3
```

Validation mode only attempts to compile the manifest and validate the syntax. It won't actually apply anything, so you can safely run this command anywhere.

You could run this check manually or via a Git hook, for example, to validate the manifest before committing it to your repository.

Debug output

When Puppet isn't doing what you expect, it can be very difficult to work out why. A time-honored debugging technique used by many programmers is to print out information at different points to show you what's going on.

Notify resources

A handy way to do this is to use a `notify` resource. We've sneaked these into the book several times so far without explaining what they are. A `notify` resource simply prints out its name to the console when you run Puppet:

```
notify { 'Got this far!': }
```

The preceding manifest produces:

```
ubuntu@demo:~/puppet$ papply
Notice: Got this far!
Notice: /Stage[main]//Node[demo]/Notify[Got this far!]/message: defined
'message' as 'Got this far!'
Notice: Finished catalog run in 0.07 seconds
```

A simple message like this can help you figure out whether Puppet is even loading or applying a particular bit of code. If you want to find out the value of a variable at a certain point in the manifest, you can interpolate it into a string, like this:

```
notify { "I think my hostname is ${::hostname}": }
```

Note that you need double quotes (`"like this"`) around the string or Puppet won't process it for variables. You'll see an output like this:

```
ubuntu@demo:~/puppet$ papply
Notice: I think my hostname is demo
Notice: /Stage[main]//Node[demo]/Notify[I think my hostname is demo]/
message: defined 'message' as 'I think my hostname is demo'
Notice: Finished catalog run in 0.06 seconds
```

Exec output

If you use an `exec` resource to run a command, and the command fails, Puppet will give you an error message including the output from the command. For example, if you have an `exec` like this:

```
exec { 'this-will-fail':
  command => '/bin/cat /tmp/doesntexist',
}
```

You'll see this output:

```
ubuntu@demo:~/puppet$ papply
Notice: /Stage[main]//Node[demo]/Exec[this-will-fail]/returns: /bin/cat:
/tmp/doesntexist: No such file or directory
```

```
Error: /bin/cat /tmp/doesntexist returned 1 instead of one of [0]
```

```
Error: /Stage[main]//Node[demo]/Exec[this-will-fail]/returns: change from
notrun to 0 failed: /bin/cat /tmp/doesntexist returned 1 instead of one
of [0]
```

```
Notice: Finished catalog run in 0.13 seconds
```

As you can see, Puppet not only reports that the command returned a failed exit status:

```
Error: /bin/cat /tmp/doesntexist returned 1 instead of one of [0]
```

But also, the actual output from running the command:

```
Notice: /Stage[main]//Node[demo]/Exec[this-will-fail]/returns: /bin/cat:
/tmp/doesntexist: No such file or directory
```

Very useful! But sometimes the command can succeed and yet whatever was supposed to happen doesn't happen. We'd like to be able to see the output of the command even though it didn't return an error. To do this, set the `logoutput` attribute of the exec to `true`:

```
exec { 'this-will-succeed-but-give-us-output-anyway':
  command   => '/bin/cat /etc/hostname',
  logoutput => true,
}
```

This will produce output such as the following:

```
ubuntu@demo:~/puppet$ papply
```

```
Notice: /Stage[main]//Node[demo]/Exec[this-will-succeed]/returns: demo
```

```
Notice: /Stage[main]//Node[demo]/Exec[this-will-succeed]/returns:
executed successfully
```

```
Notice: Finished catalog run in 0.14 seconds
```

The default value of `logoutput` is `on_failure`, which means "only show the command output if it fails." Setting it to `true` will always show the command output. If you set it to `false`, you'll never see command output even in the case of a failure.

 In older versions of Puppet, `logoutput` defaulted to `false`, so you needed to explicitly set it to `on_failure` if you wanted to see failed command output. In Puppet 3.0 and later, `on_failure` is the default.

Specifying expected exit status

How does Puppet know whether a command succeeded or failed? UNIX-like systems use a numeric value called the **exit status** to indicate this. The convention is to return an exit status of 0 if all is well, and some non-zero value if there was a problem. Some commands return different non-zero values depending on the specific error. As you can see in the example, if you try to use `cat` on a file that doesn't exist, it returns an exit status of 1.

Puppet interprets a non-zero exit status as failure, and raises an error. If you want to run a command that returns a non-zero exit status, but you're happy for Puppet to ignore this, you can specify the `returns` attribute for the `exec`, to tell Puppet what exit status to expect:

```
exec { 'this-will-fail-but-that-is-ok':
  command => '/bin/cat /tmp/doesntexist',
  returns => 1,
}
```

In this case, Puppet will only raise an error if the exit status is something other than 1.

Monitoring

Devops people like to say, "If it's not monitored, it's not in production." By "monitored," what we really mean is that some automated system is checking whatever it is, and alerting you if there's a problem. If your customers know the system is down before you do, then you don't have effective monitoring.

Managing monitoring with Puppet

Puppet can be a big help with monitoring, as it can be with all other aspects of automation and control. At the least, you can use Puppet to help you set up a monitoring server (using Nagios, Icinga, Zabbix, or one of the many other freely-available monitoring tools).

Puppet has some built-in support for Nagios in particular, and can automatically generate monitoring checks for hosts and services that you manage in your Puppet manifest. This requires **PuppetDB**, a central database that stores information about your nodes. We haven't space here to go into the details of PuppetDB and stored configuration, but you can find out more at:

```
https://puppetlabs.com/blog/introducing-puppetdb-put-your-data-to-
work/
```

What to monitor

However you manage your monitoring infrastructure, there are some basic things you will want to monitor:

◆ Hosts being alive

◆ Web sites responding to HTTP requests

◆ Processes running

◆ Memory and disk space being within limits

You can also monitor Puppet itself. This is especially useful if you are running Puppet automatically from cron, perhaps using a similar setup to that described in *Chapter 4, Managing Puppet with Git*. We'd like to know at least:

◆ Whether Puppet has run recently

◆ Whether the run succeeded or failed

We'll see how to do this in the next section.

Monitoring Puppet status

You can do this very simply by having Puppet write a file on each server when it runs. For example:

```
file { '/tmp/puppet.lastrun':
  content => inline_template('<%= Time.now %>'),
  backup  => false,
}
```

This will write the current date and time to the file /tmp/puppet.lastrun, and you can check this file with your monitoring system. If you run Puppet every 10 minutes, say, then the timestamp file should be no more than 10 minutes old. Allowing a little time for the Puppet run itself, which could take up to a few minutes, you might set your monitoring system to alert you if the file is, say, 15 minutes old.

> Did you notice that we've specified backup => false for the puppet.lastrun file? Normally, Puppet creates a backup copy of any file it changes, and stores it on the machine in a place called the **clientbucket**. This can be handy if you ever accidentally overwrite an important file, and want to retrieve its original contents. In this case, however, Puppet will be changing the file every time it runs, and we don't want to waste space storing lots of useless backup copies. backup => false tells Puppet never to back up this file.

Problems with Puppet

There are many possible reasons for an alert to be triggered by the `puppet.lastrun` file becoming too old:

- The cron job that runs Puppet didn't fire. Maybe it was disabled by someone making local changes to the machine, who then forgot to re-enable it.

- Git wasn't able to pull changes. Maybe the Git server is down, or inaccessible, or the SSH authentication got messed up. Maybe someone made local changes to the Puppet repo but then didn't commit them, causing `git pull` to complain.

- Puppet wasn't able to run. Maybe there's a typo in the manifest, or another error that means the manifest doesn't compile properly.

Whatever the reason, you'll be able to go in and investigate why Puppet isn't running, and you'll know which machines are potentially out of sync with the manifest.

Staying in sync

Some people don't like to run Puppet regularly on their machines because they worry that it might change something unexpectedly. In fact, the best way to avoid this is to run Puppet all the time. Why? Because if you don't do this, when you eventually do run Puppet on a machine, there will be lots of changes all happening at once, which makes it difficult to diagnose any problems you may have.

Also, one of the main benefits of using Puppet is that you know your machines are all in sync with each other and the manifest. If you make a change to the manifest that could potentially break something on a machine, it's better for you to find out now so you can fix it. Running Puppet with `--noop` can help you make sure that your latest changes haven't caused problems.

It's a good idea, if your budget allows, to set up some **staging servers**, and make them as similar as possible to your production systems. You can then test any changes to Puppet, package versions, configuration, or software releases on the staging servers and eliminate any problems before rolling out to production.

If you're very risk-averse, you could run Puppet automatically on the staging servers but only run it manually on the live servers when you need to push out a change.

Errors

The two main kinds of error you're likely to encounter when running Puppet are **compilation errors**—errors in the manifest itself, or in template files—and **errors from commands** executed by Puppet when applying the manifest. We'll look at these in turn.

Compilation errors

If you make a typo in the manifest, or some other kind of error, Puppet will usually alert you when you run `puppet apply` (or `puppet parser validate`). It will tell you:

- What the error was
- What source file, and line number, the error occurred in

Diagnosing errors

Let's take an example. If we apply a manifest containing a deliberate typo, like this (can you spot it?):

```
file { '/tmp/test':
  contents => 'Hello, world'
}
```

Puppet will complain with an error message:

```
ubuntu@demo:~/puppet$ papply
Error: Invalid parameter contents at /home/ubuntu/puppet/manifests/nodes.
pp:4 on node demo.compute-1.internal
```

We actually should have said `content`, not `contents`, and Puppet is quite helpful about pointing out exactly where the problem is.

Here are some other common errors you might come across, with some hints on what might cause them.

Missing file sources

A common typo is to specify a file source as:

```
puppet://modules/sudoers/sudoers
```

Instead of:

```
puppet:///modules/sudoers/sudoers
```

That is, to put a double slash (`//`) instead of a triple slash (`///`) before `modules`. We're all used to typing web URLs, which typically have a double slash.

The format of the `source` URI is actually:

```
puppet://[HOSTNAME]/modules/...
```

The optional HOSTNAME is usually omitted unless you're using a Puppet file server, so the URI just looks like this:

```
puppet:///modules/...
```

If you miss out the third slash, Puppet will think you're trying to specify a HOSTNAME where it can find the file, and complain:

```
Error: /Stage[main]//Node[demo]/File[/tmp/test]: Could not evaluate:
getaddrinfo: Name or service not known
```

```
Could not retrieve file metadata for puppet://modules/sudoers/sudoers:
getaddrinfo: Name or service not known
```

If the source URI is correctly formatted, but the source file just doesn't exist (maybe you forgot to create it), Puppet will say instead:

```
Error: /Stage[main]//Node[demo]/File[/tmp/test]: Could not evaluate:
Could not retrieve information from environment production source(s)
puppet:///modules/sudoers/sudoers
```

Missing parent directory

If you specify a file resource with a path like this:

```
file { '/tmp/testdir/test':
  content => 'Hello, world',
}
```

Puppet requires that the directory /tmp/testdir exist before it can create the file test in it. If it doesn't, you'll see an error message similar to:

```
Error: Could not set 'file' on ensure: No such file or directory - /tmp/
testdir/test.puppettmp_236 at 4:/home/ubuntu/puppet/manifests/nodes.pp
```

You might expect that Puppet would simply create any missing path components for you. Alas! there are limits to what even a robot butler can do. You have to create the parent directory as a separate resource:

```
file { '/tmp/testdir':
  ensure => directory,
}

file { '/tmp/testdir/test':
  content => 'Hello, world',
}
```

Puppet is, however, smart enough to figure out the file /tmp/testdir/test depends on the directory /tmp/testdir being created first, so you don't have to add an explicit require for this.

Mistyped command line options

If you mistype an option name on the command line, for example, putting -debug instead of --debug, Puppet gives a very puzzling error:

```
ubuntu@demo:~/puppet$ papply -debug
Error: Could not parse for environment production: Syntax error at end of
file at line 1 on node demo.compute-1.internal
```

If you see this error, check your command line!

Summary

A quick rundown of what we've learned in this chapter.

Reporting

You can get a summary report of what Puppet did on its run by using the --summarize flag with puppet apply. For more detailed reporting, enable reports by setting report=true in /etc/puppet/puppet.conf.

Puppet will write report files to (by default, but you can change this) /var/lib/puppet/reports, in a directory named after the machine's hostname. Each report file will be named according to the date and time of the Puppet run it covers.

Puppet's report files include some summary data about the run itself, and how many resources were found to be out of sync with the manifest. This is followed by a detailed list of all the resources on the server and the number of properties that were changed or out of sync for each resource.

If any resource was changed, the report will include details of each property that was changed, with its previous value and updated value.

Debug and dry-run modes

When you don't need a full report, but you do want some more detailed information on Puppet's activity, you can use the --debug flag with puppet apply. You can also see a dry-run output of what Puppet thinks is out of sync, and what it would change, by using the --noop flag.

You can check your Puppet manifest for compilation errors using the puppet parser validate command.

Printing messages

To print out debugging messages, or other information, use a `notify` resource, which simply prints out its name to the console during Puppet's run:

```
notify { "I think my hostname is ${::hostname}": }
```

Commands run via `exec` will print their output if the command returns a failed (non-zero) exit status. To see the output even if the command succeeds, set the `logoutput` attribute to true:

```
exec { 'this-will-succeed-but-give-us-output-anyway':
  command   => '/bin/cat /etc/hostname',
  logoutput => true,
}
```

If a command routinely returns a failed exit status, but you're happy for Puppet to ignore it and carry on, you can specify the exit status that should be expected using the `returns` attribute:

```
exec { 'this-will-fail-but-that-is-ok':
  command => '/bin/cat /tmp/doesntexist',
  returns => 1,
}
```

Monitoring Puppet

If you want to be able to monitor whether Puppet is running successfully on a number of machines, without having to check each one, you can have Puppet write a timestamp file every time it runs, and check this file with your monitoring system. If the file is not updated regularly, there may be a problem running Puppet on the system.

Common Puppet errors

When Puppet does encounter a problem, it will usually print out a (more or less) helpful message, including details of the error and the source file and line number where it occurred. Some common errors that you may encounter are as follows:

Could not retrieve file metadata for XXX: getaddrinfo: Name or service not known

You may have accidentally typed `puppet://modules...` in a file source instead of `puppet:///modules...`.

Could not evaluate: Could not retrieve information from environment production source(s) XXX

The source file may not be present or in the right location in the Puppet repo.

Error: Could not set 'file' on ensure: No such file or directory XXX

The file path may specify a parent directory (or directories) that doesn't exist. You can use separate file resources in Puppet to create these.

```
Could not parse for environment production: Syntax error at end of file
at line 1
```

You may have mistyped some command line options (particularly, using a single hyphen instead of a double hyphen).

10
Moving on Up

There are only two mistakes one can make on the road to truth: not going all the way and not starting.

— *Buddha*

In this chapter, you'll learn some simple principles for writing better Puppet manifests, find some resources for learning more about Puppet, and get some ideas for practical projects that will help you start putting your Puppet skills to work.

Puppet style

Just like everyone else, I want to be a nonconformist, too. But when it comes to programming, conformity is a virtue. When your code looks the same as everybody else's, it's easy to read, easy to understand, and easy to maintain. Here are some simple Puppet style tips you can adopt now to help those who work on your code in the future, including yourself.

Break out code into modules

Logical separation of your manifest into modules is a big help when it comes to understanding and maintaining your code. Although you can structure your modules any way you want—it makes no difference to Puppet—I find the best strategy is to have each module control some more or less independent chunk of functionality.

For example, if you're writing code that manages a particular customer-facing service, such as a website or an API, that could be a module. Similarly, code that manages a specific piece of software such as Apache, MySQL, or Hadoop should have its own module.

Modules can then be connected together to do useful things; for example, a module to manage Drupal might use the Apache module, the PHP module, the MySQL module, and so on. If your modules are well-structured, there should be very little duplication of code.

Refactor common code into definitions

If you find yourself repeating very similar code several times, it's a good idea to refactor the common code into a definition. For example, the following code has a lot of duplication:

```
file{ '/etc/init/foo_worker.conf':
  source => 'puppet:///modules/admin/foo_worker.upstart',
  mode    => '0755',
}

service { 'foo_worker':
  ensure   => running,
  enable   => true,
  provider => upstart,
  require  => File['/etc/init/foo_worker.conf'],
}

file{ '/etc/init/bar_worker.conf':
  source => 'puppet:///modules/admin/bar_worker.upstart',
  mode    => '0755',
}
```

```
service { 'bar_worker':
  ensure    => running,
  enable    => true,
  provider  => upstart,
  require   => File['/etc/init/bar_worker.conf'],
}

file{ '/etc/init/baz_worker.conf':
  source  => 'puppet:///modules/admin/baz_worker.upstart',
  mode    => '0755',
}

service { 'baz_worker':
  ensure    => running,
  enable    => true,
  provider  => upstart,
  require   => File['/etc/init/baz_worker.conf'],
}
```

It defines three services, foo_worker, bar_worker, and baz_worker, each with an Upstart script to manage it. The attributes are exactly the same for each of the scripts and services, so you can make this code much simpler, shorter, and clearer by refactoring it using a definition like this:

```
# Manage worker services
define worker_service() {
  file{ "/etc/init/${name}_worker.conf":
    source  => "puppet:///modules/admin/${name}_worker.upstart",
    mode    => '0755',
  }

  service { "${name}_worker":
    ensure    => running,
    enable    => true,
    provider  => upstart,
    require   => File["/etc/init/${name}_worker.conf"],
  }
}

worker_service { ['foo', 'bar', 'baz']: }
```

In other words, identify what is common to several sections of code, and extract that part into a definition. This not only makes the code easier to understand, but if you need to modify it later, you only need to change it in one place. It's also more scalable because it's easy to add another worker_service (or a hundred).

Don't take refactoring too far, though; it can overcomplicate your code. Better to have slightly repetitive code that's easy to understand and extend, than code that's elegant but difficult to follow.

Keep node declarations simple

One of the benefits of having your infrastructure managed by Puppet is that (in theory) you can look at the manifest and see what each machine does. To help with this, keep your node declarations short, clear, and descriptive. For example:

```
node 'web1' {
   include webserver
}
```

You can look at this manifest and say, "Ah! web1 is a web server." All the individual resources, modules, parameters, and other clutter are pushed down into the web server module so that the node declaration simply says what the box is for.

Another example:

```
node 'base-server' {
   include admin::basics
   include user::sysops
   include monitoring::target
}

node 'cluster660' inherits 'base-server' {
   class { 'hadoop::node':
     master => 'cluster1',
   }
}
```

Here, we have a bunch of stuff that is common to all (or most) servers:

```
include admin::basics
include user::sysops
include monitoring::target
```

We've extracted this out into a base-server declaration. There's no actual server named base-server; however, actual servers can inherit from this node declaration and get everything in it:

```
node 'cluster660' inherits 'base-server' {
```

We know what role this machine has because it includes this class:

```
class { 'hadoop::node':
```

It takes a parameter to identify the cluster master:

```
master => 'cluster1',
```

This node declaration contains only the key information that the node needs to do its job, and tells us at a glance what that job is.

If your node declarations contain business logic, or individual resources, think about refactoring these into a class or module that the node can include.

Use puppet-lint

puppet-lint is a useful tool that checks your manifest to make sure it conforms to the Puppet Labs official style guidelines, and catches a number of common problems. For example, code like this:

```
node 'demo' {
  file { "/tmp/test":
    content => 'Hello, world',
    mode => 644,
  }
}
```

The preceding code will produce the following output from puppet-lint:

```
ubuntu@demo:~/puppet$ puppet-lint manifests/nodes.pp
ERROR: trailing whitespace found on line 2
WARNING: unquoted file mode on line 4
WARNING: double quoted string containing no variables on line 2
WARNING: mode should be represented as a 4 digit octal value or symbolic mode on line 4
WARNING: indentation of => is not properly aligned on line 4
```

When we clean it up:

```
node 'demo' {
  file { '/tmp/test':
    content => 'Hello, world',
    mode    => '0644',
  }
}
```

puppet-lint maintains an approving silence:

```
ubuntu@demo:~/puppet$ puppet-lint manifests/nodes.pp
ubuntu@demo:~/puppet$
```

You can install `puppet-lint` with the following command:

```
ubuntu@demo:~/puppet$ sudo gem install puppet-lint
Successfully installed puppet-lint-0.3.2
1 gem installed
Installing ri documentation for puppet-lint-0.3.2...
Installing RDoc documentation for puppet-lint-0.3.2...
```

To find out more about `puppet-lint` and to see what tests it runs on your code, visit the site `https://github.com/rodjek/puppet-lint`

If you keep your code lint-clean (which is to say, it passes `puppet-lint` with no errors or warnings), you can be reasonably confident that it conforms to style guidelines and doesn't contain any dangerous or deprecated syntax. This will make it easier and safer to upgrade to new versions of Puppet as they're released.

It also means your code will be easier for others to understand and work on.

Make comments superfluous

> *Good code is its own best documentation.*
>
> —*Steve McConnell, 'Code Complete'*

There is a tendency to sprinkle comments liberally throughout code, often because it's not clear what the code is doing or why it's there. Instead, rewrite the code so that no comment is needed. You can do this by using a simple, logical structure for your code and choosing descriptive names for things.

Assume that anyone reading your code is familiar with Puppet (or at least as familiar as you are), so you don't need to explain how the language works:

```
# This will run a command
exec { 'do-the-stuff':
  ...
}
```

If part of your code works by complicated magic, which you feel needs explanation in comments, simply remove the magic, and rewrite the code in a simple, obvious way. Similarly, comments like this are a sign of problems:

```
# Not sure exactly why this works - DO NOT TOUCH!!
```

Cleverness, in general, is not a characteristic of robust, reliable code. Samuel Johnson advised writers, "Read over your compositions and where ever you meet with a passage which you think is particularly fine, strike it out." He would have been an early proponent of refactoring.

There are useful comments, however. A good rule of thumb for comments, as with commit messages, is "Not what, but why." Why is this piece of code necessary?

```
# apache2-utils gives us rotatelogs
package { "apache2-utils": ensure => installed }
```

Puppet learning resources

There are several helpful web and print resources that you should keep handy when working with Puppet. This is a small selection of those that I find most useful.

Reference

It might seem obvious, but one of the best sources of reference documentation for Puppet is the Puppet Labs site itself. To save you a lot of clicking around, here are the links you'll probably use the most.

Resource types

One link that I keep bookmarked at all times is the **Puppet Type Reference**:

```
http://docs.puppetlabs.com/references/latest/type.html
```

This lists each of the types of Puppet resources—file, exec, user, and so on—with a complete description of all the attributes of each resource and what they do. Each resource also has a breakdown of the features supported by its providers or platforms.

Puppet also has some built-in help on resource types, available via the puppet describe command. For example:

```
ubuntu@demo:~/puppet$ puppet describe --list
These are the types known to puppet:
augeas            - Apply a change or an array of changes to the ...
computer          - Computer object management using DirectorySer ...
cron              - Installs and manages cron jobs
exec              - Executes external commands
file              - Manages files, including their content, owner ...
...
```

```
ubuntu@demo:~/puppet$ puppet describe file

file
====
Manages files, including their content, ownership, and permissions.

...


Parameters
----------
- **backup**
    Whether files should be backed up before
    being replaced.
```

Language and syntax

Also very important is the **Puppet Language Reference**:

```
http://docs.puppetlabs.com/puppet/3/reference/lang_summary.html
```

This describes every part of the Puppet language and syntax: variables, classes, data types, and so on. If you need to check how a particular Puppet construct works, or find out what's available, this is an excellent place to look.

Facts

For working with Facter, use the **Core Facts Reference**:

```
http://docs.puppetlabs.com/facter/latest/core_facts.html
```

This lists all of the standard facts that you can use to get information about machines, such as `fqdn`, `memorysize`, `operatingsystem`, and so on.

Style

The official Puppet Labs style guidelines (as implemented by `puppet-lint`, for example) are here:

```
http://docs.puppetlabs.com/guides/style_guide.html
```

You may not agree with all of the style rules (I'm not crazy about some of them), but there are advantages to using standard coding style. If your organization's coding style is different, or you need to break the rules for some other reason, go ahead, but it's always good to know what rules you're breaking.

Modules and code

One of the best ways to learn to write code is to look at other people's code, at least, if it's any good.

Puppet Forge

The **Puppet Forge** is a community repository of Puppet code:

```
http://forge.puppetlabs.com/
```

There you can find open source modules for managing things such as Apache, MySQL, MongoDB, Ganglia, Sphinx, and many others. These can be very useful to look at and get ideas from. In some cases you may be able to download and use the module directly in your infrastructure as is; most of the time, you will need to adapt and modify the code a little to work in your environment.

Be warned that the code on Puppet Forge is of variable quality. Some modules are excellent, mature, highly portable, well-documented, and up to date. Others aren't. Often it's quickest, easiest, and best to simply write your own code. This has the additional advantage that you learn more about Puppet while you're doing it.

A quick way to find out whether there is any Puppet Forge code relevant to what you're working on is to use the `puppet module search` command:

```
ubuntu@demo:~/puppet$ puppet module search memcached
Notice: Searching https://forge.puppetlabs.com ...
NAME            DESCRIPTION AUTHOR KEYWORDS
saz-memcached  UNKNOWN      @saz    debian redhat fedora ubuntu memcached
```

The Puppet Cookbook

If you've enjoyed this book, you might consider *The Puppet Cookbook*, by the same author:

```
http://bitfieldconsulting.com/cookbook
```

The book is aimed at those who have some familiarity with Puppet (perhaps those who've worked their way through the *Puppet Beginner's Guide*) and outlines a number of specific techniques and recipes for doing things with Puppet:

◆ Managing virtual machines with Vagrant
◆ Building a Nagios monitoring server
◆ Using Augeas to edit config files
◆ Managing users with virtual resources

- Managing Rails applications
- Managing package and gem repositories
- Managing firewalls with iptables
- Building high-availability servers with Heartbeat
- Using HAProxy for load balancing
- Using tools such as MCollective, Dashboard, and Foreman

The book contains lots of complete, working code to do all the things above and many more. As in this book, each piece of code is explained line-by-line so that you can see how it works, and use the same ideas in your own Puppet code.

It also shows you many of the tips, tricks, ideas, and advanced techniques that I've picked up over many years of working with Puppet, and that there wasn't room to cover in this book, such as:

- Using Rake to manage Puppet workflows
- Producing HTML documentation for your manifests
- Using tags, run stages, and environments
- Using class inheritance and overriding
- Importing data from commands and comma-separated values (CSV) files
- Creating custom facts
- Creating custom types and providers
- Generating manifests automatically
- Using external node classifiers

Projects

The best way to learn is by doing, so here are some things you might like to try to do with Puppet that will improve your skills and your infrastructure at the same time. Most of these projects are fairly small—a few hours of work, maybe—but each will give you a valuable win and make your life easier. They provide a series of stepping-stones from your first use of Puppet to a completely automated environment.

Puppet everywhere

Project: First, install Puppet on all the machines you're responsible for. Set up a central Git repo as described in *Chapter 4, Managing Puppet with Git*, and have each of the machines pull from the repo and run Puppet automatically. For now, Puppet won't actually manage anything, so all your node declarations will look like this:

```
node 'kermit' {
}
```

That's fine. Once you've got Puppet everywhere, you can start adding things to it.

Win: It's now easy to add configuration to any machine, simply by putting something in its node declaration.

User accounts

Project: Create a base node definition that which every machine inherits, as described earlier in this chapter in the *Keep node declarations simple* section. To this base node, add your own user account and SSH key as described in *Chapter 5, Managing Users*. You probably want to give yourself full `sudo` privileges as well. Add any other users who need login access to machines.

Win: You can now easily log in to every machine using your own named account and key, and run commands with root privileges using `sudo`.

System toolbox

Project: Add a set of packages to your base node containing software that you find useful for system administration: for example, `htop`, `dstat`, `iptraf`, `tmux`, `mosh`, `vim`, and so on. If you have custom configurations for any of these, add the config files to Puppet.

Win: You now have a well-equipped sysadmin environment on every machine, configured the way you want it.

Time sync

Project: Use Puppet to add the NTP service to all of your machines and set them to the UTC time zone. If you have a central NTP server, or your ISP does, configure `ntp.conf` to use this.

Win: All server clocks are now in sync and in the same time zone, which prevents a variety of obscure problems, and makes troubleshooting much easier (you can cross-reference timestamps in logfiles, for example).

Monitoring server

Project: If you don't already have a monitoring server such as Icinga, set one up to monitor your machines as described in *Chapter 9, Reporting and Troubleshooting*. You don't have to automate the install of Icinga for now, but have Puppet manage the list of hosts to monitor (`hosts.cfg` for Icinga) and the list of services to check (`services.cfg`).

Win: You now have automated monitoring and you can see the state of your network at a glance, including whether any hosts are down. In the future, it'll be easy to add new hosts and services to your monitoring system.

Puppetize your key services

Project: Use Puppet to manage the most important service provided by your machines.

Your priorities for bringing services under Puppet management should be driven by business considerations. What service or facility is most critical or earns the most money for your business? Or, if you're a non-profit, the most business for your business?

Once you've decided on the most important thing to Puppetize, make a list of exactly what needs to be managed. For example, if it's a website, you might list the following things to be managed by Puppet:

- Web server installed
- Virtual host file to serve website
- Directory where site is deployed
- Database for website

The list should contain everything you would have to do manually to set up a new server to serve the website (not including, for example, installing the operating system, since Puppet requires that, too). You probably also won't include deploying the website itself, unless it consists of just a few static files. What Puppet needs do to is make the machine ready to have the site deployed to it, whatever the deployment process is (FTP, Capistrano, shell scripts, and so on).

Don't attempt to have Puppet manage these things on the existing live server. Instead, set up a new server and build up the configuration, checking against the live machine as you go to make sure you have included everything. Then it's easy to know when you're done; when you can deploy the site to the new machine and it works identically to the live version, you're done.

You can turn down or repurpose the old machine (keep it around for a little while, though, just in case there's something you missed).

Win: Your key service is under Puppet management, and that service can now be easily and quickly built on a new server if anything happens to the live one. Also, you have complete documentation for what's required to run it.

Automate backups

Project: Use Puppet to distribute backup scripts to each machine and run backup jobs automatically via cron. You should have a local copy of all important data (that is, in a backup directory on the machine) and an offsite copy of anything that can't easily be reconstructed. This should be off the machine, off your infrastructure, and out of your ISP's data center (Amazon S3 is one option).

Monitor the backup jobs with your monitoring server (have the job write a logfile, and you can monitor that the logfile has been touched, and doesn't contain any error messages).

Use Puppet to build copies of your machines and test restoring the data to them. Write down the procedure you follow to do this, so that someone else could follow it, and put the procedure document where it can be easily found. Knowledge of the restore procedure shouldn't die with you.

Win: Your data (and thus your business) is no longer a hostage to fortune. You needn't just hope that your hard disks won't fail, or that your ISP won't lose connectivity. In fact, no sentence that contains the word "hope" is part of a viable operations strategy.

Set up staging servers

Project: Once you've fully Puppetized a server, create a "staging" version that is identical to the live version. When you need to test upgrades, new releases, or changes to the setup, you can try them out on the staging server first and avoid any unexpected problems in production.

Win: You have a staging environment where you can try out changes (no more committing and hoping). Also, it's easy to create copies of your live server, for redundancy, load balancing, or development VMs.

Automate everything

Project: Extend Puppet management to any remaining parts of your infrastructure that still require manual setup. For any particular machine or service, ask yourself this question:

If I wipe and reinstall this machine, then run Puppet, will it be in production?

If the answer is *No*, then you still have some work to do. If the answer is *Yes*, then do the test to make sure. (It might be wise to use a replacement server rather than wiping the live one and finding you can't rebuild it.)

If there are manual steps that you can't automate or do without (restoring data from a backup, say), write down a detailed procedure for what has to be done, so that someone else could follow it. Write down what you need to type, what you'll see, error messages you might encounter, and so on.

Your written procedures are business-critical software just like your application source code. Procedures are just software that runs on humans. Write, test, and maintain procedures with as much care and pride as you do your computer software.

Win: You can spend less time on day-to-day operations matters, such as building and configuring servers, and you can concentrate on really valuable tasks, such as making your systems faster, more resilient, and more cost-effective.

You have more time to communicate with your colleagues, instead of computers.

You can make infrastructure changes quickly and safely, making the business more agile.

You have time for training, learning, research, experimentation, and innovation.

You can share your knowledge with others by helping them use Puppet to achieve what they need to do. In the process, you'll learn expertise from them about their own domains and specialties.

Last word

System administration can be a rather conservative profession. ("If it ain't broke, don't fix it.") Worse, some system administrators suffer from an attitude problem. Perhaps they perceive themselves as undervalued by colleagues, like a kind of digital janitor. Perhaps they're reluctant to share what they know, for fear of making themselves dispensable. Perhaps they're simply so overloaded with time-consuming work that their default response is "Go away!"

This can lead to "BOFH": the system administrator as remote, unfriendly, inaccessible, enforcing unhelpful and bureaucratic policies, rejecting new ideas. The last person, in fact, you'd want to ask for help with a problem.

Automation tools such as Puppet are a threat to this kind of sysadmin, because she sees herself as the guardian of the secret technical information about how the systems work. "Why, if all that information was in Puppet, everyone would be able to see and understand it, and they could build and manage their own servers! Then I wouldn't be needed!"

Obviously, this isn't you, or you wouldn't be reading this book (unless someone bought it for you and left it on your desk, pointedly highlighting this section). But if you know someone who fits that description, share this with them:

- The more you automate the tedious parts of your job, the more time you have for the exciting and challenging parts. You know, the ones that need a brain

- The more opportunity you have to use your brain, the more you can learn about and explore new technologies and ideas

- The more automated your systems, the more quickly you can deliver new things, and the more you can be known as the person who solves problems, instead of creating them

- The more you can innovate, improve the status quo, and add value for the business, the more indispensable you'll be to the business

- The more you share your knowledge, teach, and inspire others, the more your colleagues will value you, and the higher the opinion they'll have of your skills and expertise. And that won't go unnoticed by whoever signs your paycheck

So go to it! And have fun.

Index

Symbols

A

B

C

H

hashes
 about 138, 142
 hash keys, testing 139
 multilevel hashes 138
hasstatus 45
home attribute 74
hostname 101

I

if statements 124
infrastructure as code 13
inline_template function 101
installing, Puppet
 prerequisites 22
 steps for 23, 24, 25
ipaddress 101
issues
 about 8
 solving 11

J

jen user 17
jobs
 running, as specified user 94
 running, at regular intervals 94
 scheduled 104

K

key 138

L

logical expression 128

M

magnitude, comparisons 129
manifest
 about 18, 26, 31
 applying 27
 changing 56-59
 directory structure, creating 29
 distributing 61
 existing files, modifying 28

 importing, in Git 55, 56
 nodes.pp file, creating 29, 30
 organizing 28
 Puppet, applying 26
 reliability 61
 scalability 61
 simplicity 61
master Git repo
 creating 62, 63
master repo
 changes, pushing to 65, 66
 cloning, to new machine 63-65
memorysize 101
messages
 printing 161
modules
 about 38, 50
 code, breaking into 164
 Nginx module, creating 38, 39
monitoring
 about 155
 managing, with puppet 155
 puppet 161
 puppet status 156
MSI images
 installing, from Puppet Labs website 25
multilevel hash 138, 142

N

Nginx
 installing 34
nginx class 116
Nginx module
 creating 38, 39
Nginx service
 adding 41
Nginx websites
 definition, creating for 113, 114
node
 adding 65
 declarations 166, 167
node declaration
 about 29, 32
 creating 30
node definitions 135, 136

Thank you for buying
Puppet 3 Beginner's Guide

About Packt Publishing

Packt, pronounced 'packed', published its first book "*Mastering phpMyAdmin for Effective MySQL Management*" in April 2004 and subsequently continued to specialize in publishing highly focused books on specific technologies and solutions.

Our books and publications share the experiences of your fellow IT professionals in adapting and customizing today's systems, applications, and frameworks. Our solution based books give you the knowledge and power to customize the software and technologies you're using to get the job done. Packt books are more specific and less general than the IT books you have seen in the past. Our unique business model allows us to bring you more focused information, giving you more of what you need to know, and less of what you don't.

Packt is a modern, yet unique publishing company, which focuses on producing quality, cutting-edge books for communities of developers, administrators, and newbies alike. For more information, please visit our website: www.packtpub.com.

About Packt Open Source

In 2010, Packt launched two new brands, Packt Open Source and Packt Enterprise, in order to continue its focus on specialization. This book is part of the Packt Open Source brand, home to books published on software built around Open Source licences, and offering information to anybody from advanced developers to budding web designers. The Open Source brand also runs Packt's Open Source Royalty Scheme, by which Packt gives a royalty to each Open Source project about whose software a book is sold.

Writing for Packt

We welcome all inquiries from people who are interested in authoring. Book proposals should be sent to author@packtpub.com. If your book idea is still at an early stage and you would like to discuss it first before writing a formal book proposal, contact us; one of our commissioning editors will get in touch with you.

We're not just looking for published authors; if you have strong technical skills but no writing experience, our experienced editors can help you develop a writing career, or simply get some additional reward for your expertise.

Puppet 2.7 Cookbook

ISBN: 978-1-84951-538-2   Paperback: 300 pages

Build reliable, scalable, secure, high-performance systems to fully utilize the power of cloud computing

1. Shows you how to use 100 powerful advanced features of Puppet, with detailed step-by-step instructions

2. Covers all the popular tools and frameworks used with Puppet: Dashboard, Foreman, MCollective, and more

3. Includes the latest features and updates in Puppet 2.7

Instant Puppet 3 Starter

ISBN: 978-1-78216-174-5   Paperback: 50 pages

Gain complete consistency from your systems with minimal effort using Instant Puppet 3 Starter

1. Learn something new in an Instant! A short, fast, focused guide delivering immediate results.

2. Learn how deterministic results can vastly reduce your workload

3. Deploy Puppet Server as a Ruby-on-Rails application to handle thousands of clients

Please check **www.PacktPub.com** for information on our titles

CPSIA information can be obtained at www.ICGtesting.com
Printed in the USA
LVOW09s0951050715

445010LV00010B/348/P